Praise for *Write from the Heart*

"Combines insight, experience, and ancient wisdom in a surprisingly personal and accessible guide to writing. Not only worth reading but referencing and studying."   — Hugh Prather

"This is a writing course that doesn't seem like learning. It feels like an adventure."   — Tom Squirer, *Looks at Books*

"This is not a book on standard writing technique.... It is instead a guide to — and meditation on — writing as a path to the soul."
                                         — Richard Heinberg, *Intuition Magazine*

"Altogether, this is a satisfying book that should be provocative and engaging for all kinds of writers, published or not.
                                         — Krysta Gibson, *The New Times*

"...woven together with an easy flow. I learned much about connecting with that flow and expanding myself as a writer."
                                         — Susan Warrick, *Magical Blend*

"Highly recommended for anyone who writes — whether for personal journaling practice or for publication by the professional writer with years of experience."   — Kathy Prata, *Branches Reviews*

"Inspirational and intimate, this book resonates with literary and spiritual truths."   — Meera Lester, *Writers Connection*

"For anyone who has ever dreamed of becoming a published author, *Write from the Heart* should be looked upon as required reading."
                                         — *Evolving Woman*

"Offers writers an informative, personal conversation on the intricacies of getting the heart down on the page…an especially good guide for those wondering where their stories really begin."

— *Evolving Times*

"Beginning as well as accomplished writers will delight in Bennett's words." — *NAPRA ReView*

"Don't miss this in-depth exploration of writing from your heart and tapping your own lifetime supply of creativity."

— *Writers Digest Book Club Bulletin*

"A gifted author, Hal Bennett shares his personal process and describes what each of us can do to remove the blocks to our own creativity and thus more fully express our essential being — the wise, loving, powerful, creative entity that we are at our core."

— Shakti Gawain, author of *Creative Visualization*

"Write from the Heart offers a new way to look at writing . . . reminding us that through the miracle of language we can embrace and share the wisdom of our hearts."

— Jerry Jampolsky, M.D., author of *Love Is Letting Go of Fear*

"Hal Zina Bennett practices writing as a spiritual path. He teaches with the compassion and wisdom born of experience and humility. Writers, and those who wish to be, are well served by his insight, candor, and humor — one of the handful of real writing books."

— Julia Cameron, author of *The Artist's Way*

WRITE FROM
THE HEART

Other Books by Hal Zina Bennett

Follow Your Bliss

The Lens of Perception

Spirit Circle (fiction)

Spirit Animals & The Wheel of Life

The Well Body Book

White Mountain Blues (fiction)

Zuni Fetishes

WRITE FROM THE HEART

Revised Edition

Unleashing
the Power of Your
Creativity

Hal Zina Bennett

NATARAJ PUBLISHING

a division of

NEW WORLD LIBRARY
NOVATO, CALIFORNIA

Nataraj Publishing

a division of

 New World Library
14 Pamaron Way
Novato, California 94949

Copyright © 1995, 2001 by Hal Zina Bennett
Cover design: Mary Beth Salmon
Text design and typosgraphy: Tona Pearce Myers

Library of Congress Cataloging-in-Publication Data
    Bennett, Hal Zina, 1936–
    Write from the heart : unleashing the power of your creativity /
    Hal Zina Bennett.—Rev. ed.
       p.   cm.
    Includes bibliographical references.
    ISBN 1-57731-177-9
    1. Authorship. 2. Creative ability. I. Title.
PN151.B514 2001
808'.02—dc21   00-062217

ISBN 1-57731-177-9
First printing, February 2001
Printed in Canada on recycled, acid-free paper
Distributed to the trade by Publishers Group West

10 9 8 7 6 5 4 3

Dedicated to Susan J. Sparrow,

for her patience and humor,

but mostly for her quiet wisdom,

constant love, and partnership

Contents

ACKNOWLEDGMENTS

No book is the work of the author alone. Rather, behind the scenes there's a closely knit team of dedicated folks who make it all happen. Though some of us have never met, your contribution has not gone unappreciated.

Thanks to Jason Gardner, my editor at New World Library, for your steady hand, creative suggestions, professionalism, and good book talk.

Thanks to Ryan Madden who researched the needs of new writers.

Thanks to Tona Pearce Myers for a type design that makes reading a pleasure and to Mary Beth Salmon for a new cover design that flies across the room.

Thank you to Barbara King and Annelise Zamula for copyediting and proofreading.

I want to thank Jane Hogan and Shakti Gawain who first saw the promise of this book.

Marc Allen and Munro Magruder, I am indebted to you for your enthusiastic support of this new edition, and for your dedication to one of the most admirable publishing missions in the business today.

Finally, and most fondly, my special thanks to the thousands of readers, students, clients, and friends who have helped me probe and better understand the inner workings of the creative process. And my deep appreciation for suggestions and feedback from our *Write from the Heart* mentors throughout the U.S.

Thank you all!

PREFACE

———————————

I wonder sometimes where the writing of a book begins. Probably it starts somewhere soon after our birth, even before we have mastered the art of language. While that may be so, I see this one as having begun sometime after that, approximately thirty years ago, when I began teaching creative writing and coaching other writers through the birth of their projects. Some 200-plus successful projects later, and a half-dozen best-sellers among them, I felt that maybe I knew enough about this demanding craft to write a book about it.

If you were to ask me what is the most important thing I have to teach about writing, it would be this: that when we try to learn how to write by studying the craft, we are probably putting the proverbial cart before the horse. After all, craft grows out of observing what we do when we speak or write from our most authentic self — when we write from the heart. We do not learn how to do that by studying craft.

But what if there were a way to learn the craft of writing from the heart? That's the question I asked in writing this book, and if those who have read it are any measure, I would have to say that this effort has been more than moderately successful. The book — or rather, my readers, students, and clients — have proved that writing can be taught this way. They have proved that knowing how to access the stuff of the heart, and knowing how to honor our own life experiences through our writing, almost automatically leads to craft.

When humans started telling stories, gathered around fires tens of thousands of years ago, they did not have books or teachers to show them the craft. Instead, they found that the truth of the storyteller holds the listener's attention. Magic happens when the story rises out of the teller's own life, and most listeners recognize this immediately. So does the storyteller, of course, for she or he measures it in ecstasy. The space between writer and reader, teller and listener, suddenly dissolves. The story itself can be made up, and usually is, but the energy and vividness and style of the telling rises from the heart, which has in turn been molded by the life experiences of the storyteller.

It has often been said that the best writers are born, not made. What I have observed, however, is something a little different than what this homily seems to imply. I prefer to think that good writing cannot be taught by teaching craft alone. But I do think that people can learn to be good, maybe even great, writers by learning to write from the heart. And that is the promise of this book.

— H. Z. B, October 2000

In Search
of the Creative Source

Every secret of a writer's soul, every experience of his life,
every quality of his mind is written large in his works....

— Virginia Woolf

Friends who knew me in my childhood tell me I was a very strange little boy. Some say this is how writers are supposed to begin their lives. Maybe so. I spent those early years in the suburbs of Detroit, back when most Midwestern suburbs were still surrounded by working farms, open fields, and relatively untouched stretches of woodlands and wetlands. My parents built their dream home on a quiet road, way beyond sidewalks and paved streets. It was one of those idealized mid-American neighborhoods, with white picket fences and antique lanterns mounted on white painted posts to announce the house numbers. Even our street name invoked the ideals of that time: Pleasant Avenue.

The narrow road that went by our house was oiled gravel, which meant that once or twice a year a grungy truck from the county lumbered through our neighborhood, spraying watery, black creosote on the gravel to keep down the summer dust. Although my father drove thirty miles to a city job every day, we also had our half acre of land, where we kept a few laying hens and planted a vegetable garden every spring.

Judging by my own memory and the stories I've been told, I lived in a world all my own. I was a dreamer. My parents were afraid that someday I'd get hit by a car for lack of proper attention to the real world. I remember it differently. I recall things like climbing trees in the forested area behind our home and just sitting there, ensconced on a limb thirty feet above the ground, rocked by a gentle breeze. I noticed early on that when I immersed myself in that world, surrounded by nature, and didn't move a muscle, birds and other wildlife no longer noticed me and would go about their business as if I wasn't there. When that happened, my attention shifted and I became very still inside, particularly in the spring and early fall when I could nestle in, hugging the barky trunk, looking out through a curtain of brightly colored leaves.

It isn't that I was all that interested in nature, at least not consciously so. More than anything else, I enjoyed the profound solitude of those moments, away from the house, where it seemed there was always a level of busyness that took me too far out of myself. Years later, when I first read Robert Frost's poem "Birches," I immediately knew what he meant when he talked about the boy who grew up "too far from town to learn baseball, / Whose only play was what he found himself...." Even though I wasn't far from town, I never did learn baseball, no doubt because other things interested me more. I regretted that at times, mostly when I was excluded from neighborhood games and sulked back home with my head down. But I continued to find greater satisfaction and excitement in the creative process, long before I even knew enough to call it that.

When I look back and relive those early years, I begin to appreciate what good training they were for a writer. First, I think, they impressed upon me a deep appreciation for the sumptuous luxuries of solitude, too often neglected in the frenzy of modern life. And second, those years gave me time to unhurriedly explore the magic of the inner world, from which we draw the themes and rich imagery that give our creative efforts their originality.

If those years served me well, they also taught me something that has been invaluable in my work with other writers. It is that most of the skills required by this craft are pretty commonplace. And the magic ingredients so many of us writers seek, that will allow us to turn our dreams of becoming successful writers into the real thing, are always right there under our noses. And it all starts with solitude, with the experience of sitting quietly until we are welcomed into our own inner worlds.

As simple as that sounds, it's also something that we trade off for the lesser pleasures of modern life, like the portable radios that you see people wearing on their heads, even on hiking trails in the wilderness. I often wonder if learning solitude wouldn't, in the long run, be a better skill to teach schoolchildren than grammar exercises and algebra, which most of us forget all too quickly anyhow. Although my parents always assured me that I was offered excellent educational opportunities — the implication being that I hadn't taken advantage of them — I cannot recall a single teacher who even suggested that there was any value to be found in solitude. On the contrary, people who spent too much time looking inward were not to be wholly trusted and were generally thought to be just a step or two from the funny farm.

When I sat down to write this book, I knew that the central message I had to convey to other writers was that the most valuable asset we have in this vocation is ourselves. Even the best writers seem to require constant reminders of that. There are a million books out there that teach writing techniques: how to create characters, how to develop a focused theme, how to write dialogue, or how to organize your book. All of this has its place, of course, but I also know that I share the frustration of other people who finish reading books of that kind, or come away from writing workshops that focus on techniques, longing for something more.

The something more I always wanted when I was first starting out had to do with questions like: Where do I look for the imagery and themes I can feel truly passionate about? Where do I find ideas so thoroughly engaging that the sheer momentum of my fascination will propel me forward, to fill the three or four hundred pages it takes to make a book? And finally, How can I truly make a contribution through my writing? What are my gifts? What is my mission?

When we love books, it's doubly difficult to answer these questions. We wander through the aisles of our favorite bookstore and think, "Is there really anything new under the sun? Is there really something I have to add to all this?" I must confess that walking through the library stacks, or even searching through my own helter-skelter bookshelves, I ask those same questions. Certainly many minds have far more to say than I. But when I start feeling sorry for myself, vowing that I will never write another word, I hear the voice of the spiritual teacher who told me, "There is nothing new under the sun — except you!"

His point was that each of us who dares to reach in and pull out what is truly ourselves brings a new way of seeing into the world. You may not be saying something that multitudes before you haven't said, but the way you say it, the particular spin you put on it, colored and tempered by your own unique life experience, allows some to hear it for the first time. And that's the only justification I have ever found for climbing out on that precarious swaying limb that writing requires of us.

"To thine own self be true" is probably the oldest and most ubiquitous saying in all the world's religious and philosophical teaching. And there's no doubt in my mind that the profession of writing calls on us to do that over and over again. Being true to ourselves is what gives our writing fire. It's what lights our lights when we're reading. But it's also the one thing we humans are only beginning to learn.

I believe that you don't have to be an expert at the art of self-knowledge to be a good writer — or a good person, for that matter. Being true to ourselves about 10 percent of the time seems about as close as most of us ever get. And that seems to be enough. That 10 percent, like the infinitesimal specks of pollen that cling to a bee's proboscis, can beautify and nourish the world if we dare risk it.

Over the past three decades that I've been writing and coaching other authors, I've seen a new style of writing emerge in fiction, nonfiction, poetry, and journaling that uses these lessons about self-truths in a new way. It seems that we're finally recognizing that nobody can ever be the final authority on anything.

To share our humanness — that is, what we've encountered on our own life path — turns out to be far more valuable than claiming we have discovered ultimate truths or even that we've come up with something truly original.

If this book does nothing else, I hope that it says something to every reader about the process of opening to our own uniqueness. I hope that it shines some light on the often hidden part within each one of us that holds the rich imagery, themes, life experiences, and wizardry that make writing such a powerful medium. Study writing technique, but never forget, even for a moment, to be true to yourself, to honor the wondrous treasures you embody.

More and more people are seeking ways to open the gates to their own creativity. And many have found that writing can do that for them. Even in the past ten years, men and women from all walks of life have become enchanted by the power of words and the inner worlds we can discover through them. Some write novels, some write poetry, some write nonfiction, while others are content to confine their work to their private journals. I have found it fascinating to watch this great groundswell of interest in writing and creativity, and I think it is no accident that this interest in writing has paralleled what has been called a spiritual renaissance. We are all seeking greater meaning in our lives, and for many people creativity represents a kind of golden grail, promising a sense of personal fulfillment and healing that nothing else can.

I like what Matthew Fox said about it: "Creativity is the link between our inner work and the outer work that society requires of us. Creativity is the threshold through which our nonaction leads to actions of beautification, celebration, and healing in the world. Creativity is both an inner work and an outer work."

One thing is certain: Few of us any longer think of creativity as a frivolous activity, or as something only self-indulgent, "arty" people take seriously. We're recognizing that it nurtures us, at a time when humanity is very much in need of spiritual support. We're realizing that our creative efforts are a way to bring us all a little closer to ourselves and, in doing so, renew the spirit of humankind.

As a professional writer, creative writing teacher, and writing coach for more than thirty-five years, I have known and helped a lot of writers, ranging from those who are just beginning to those who have written international best-sellers that made them millionaires. But the thing that has most interested me through all of it is having them reveal to me their private thoughts about what they believed to be the vital sources of their creativity.

It is clear to me that those who have been most successful in writing have been men and women who recognized the gift of their own life experiences and discovered how to shape that material into artifacts that could make a lasting impact on their readers. There is, after all, nothing we can hope to know better than our own life experiences. Buckminster Fuller once said, "I am the only guinea pig I have," suggesting something the creative person understands only too well, that everything that happens to us is potentially the raw material for anything we might one day wish to write. While Fuller was addressing a convention of engineers, his idea perhaps applies even more accurately to writers.

There are great mysteries spun around what many have described as our "creative wellsprings," the source from which our passions, our inspiration, and our imagery come. Too often, the subject of creativity and inspiration leaves us more bewildered than informed, with the impression that the creative spirit is a distant angel who has to be teased into our lives, manipulated and seduced into serving us. Having worked with literally hundreds of writers over the years, I am convinced that our most powerful creative sources are far more accessible, and incidentally, far more down to earth than this.

We each have within us many characters — children, adults, playmates, animals, wise counselors. The cast of characters is seemingly infinite. We have only to consider our dreams, peopled with characters of all shapes, sizes, colors, and convictions, for evidence that this is true. Through our exploration of this inner world we each find the roots of our unique voice and our creativity. And yet, in a way that is practically impossible to explain, once having attained our own voice and learned to draw from our own creative source, we see and hear not only how we are each unique but how we are all the same. We glimpse the single, unifying consciousness that makes us one. What is most idiosyncratically you allows us to look beyond what is most idiosyncratically me, so together we can view the stillpoint where our experience of life is exactly the same.

In our creative and spiritual lives, I am convinced there is such a thing as divine inspiration. It is undoubtedly the most powerful source of our creativity. Even this is accessible to all of us, however. I have watched writers of every age and expertise tap into this source — surprising even themselves — by concentrating on the very personal and individual sources we're exploring here.

If all this seems a bit obscure, don't worry. The stories I'll share with you in the pages to come will make these ideas more accessible. I have learned many processes — I hate calling them "techniques" — to use in my own writing, and I have passed these along to the hundreds of writers I've helped to develop successful projects over the years. Whenever possible, I'll share their stories with you. I think these stories are at least as valuable as my own. When you take all these anecdotes as a whole, this book, in effect, turns out to be a chorus of voices, collectively much bigger than my own. I trust that our songs will inspire you to join in!

HOW TO USE THIS BOOK

If you have already flipped through these pages, you have probably noticed the instructive sections I call "Writing Explorations" at the ends of chapters one through eleven. In addition to these new exercises, this revised edition of the book includes sidebar quotations from other writers to help underscore ideas in the adjacent text. You will see other sidebars, labeled "Core Concepts," that help to succinctly focus each chapter's theme. These are strategically placed in each chapter to help bring difficult ideas into sharp focus.

The "Writing Explorations" are experiential exercises. They grew out of our Write from the Heart seminars and from my own experiences as an author, writing coach, and editor for the past thirty-five years.

You can approach these exercises in two ways. If you are the type of person who prefers to read the text, you can simply ignore the exercises and read straight through. If experiential exercises help you to integrate new ideas with your own, you can pause and complete the exercises as you read.

Like our seminars, the "Writing Explorations" are designed to help you find your own creative resources and unique writing voice.

In many cases these exercises demand a lot — but they also produce a lot, as any graduate from our writing seminars will tell you.

You'll find that the exercises work cumulatively — that is, each successive exercise builds on the others. In that respect, they are much more than warmups or suggested writing themes. They will put you right into the heart of the creative process, demanding that you draw from your deepest resources and calling you to raise your own unique voice.

If you're planning to complete the exercises, I recommend that you keep your work in a journal. It will make an excellent, ongoing reference to aid your growth as a writer.

DAILY MEDITATION EXERCISE
WRITING IN THE PRESENT

Even if you do no other assignments in this book, do this one. Do it daily, religiously, and it will teach you everything you need to know about tapping the richest vein of your creative resources. When we started Write from the Heart Mentor's Groups in 1996, writing in the present became nearly everyone's daily writing discipline. Even if they wrote nothing else, they did this, dating their work and keeping it in bound journals so that they could return to their material. In many cases, poems, short stories, and even whole books grew out of what was originally practiced as a simple daily exercise.

You will quickly notice in doing this writing meditation, either as your morning writing or in the evening, that this is not random writing. Just as with Zen meditation, it takes you to the core of your consciousness in each particular moment. And as you write, you discover a great deal about yourself, how you focus your attention, and the life themes that consistently capture your attention.

The assignment is deceptively simple:

1. Sit down with your journal and write down as closely and engagingly as you can exactly what is happening to

you in the present. If you have trouble getting started, begin with these words: "I am now putting my hands on the keyboard..." or "...pen to paper." Then proceed, describing as closely as you can the environment and your response to it in the immediate present. (Warning: This exercise is actually impossible to do literally, as you wouldn't be able to keep up even with the words flashing on the screen or the squiggles making letters on the page if you are writing in a journal.)

2. After writing for several minutes, read your writing and make note of (a) where your thoughts are taking you, (b) your awareness of your immediate environment, and (c) how you feel.

3. Write for up to ten minutes and stop. If your writing has inspired you to write something more, by all means do it!

Note: This is also a wonderful warmup exercise when you feel blocked or uninspired. For more about this exercise, see chapter seven.

CHAPTER ONE

Born to Write

When we choose a goal and invest ourselves in it to the limits of our concentration, whatever we do will be enjoyable. And once we have tasted this joy, we will redouble our efforts to taste it again. This is the way the self grows.

— Mihaly Csikszentmihalyi

Every once in a while someone asks me if I think there's such a thing as born writers. Although I suppose there are, my bet would be they are few and far between. I know I wouldn't count myself as one. Most writers I know regard their abilities as being pretty hard won, certainly not something they came into life knowing. The closest I've been to anyone who believes they were born into writing is my friend Ken who says there was a moment in his childhood when he knew he was predestined to be an author. At ten he won a library competition for a short story he wrote.

They gave him a fifty-dollar U.S. Savings Bond and a little bronze plaque with his name and the title of his story etched on it.

Ken's story was published in his hometown newspaper, along with a photograph of him clutching the plaque to his chest with his right hand and holding up the savings bond with his left. His English teacher took him aside the Monday after he got his award and encouraged him to pursue a career in journalism, telling him how terrible it would be if he wasted his God-given talent. Even then he considered journalism to be selling himself short because he'd always dreamed of writing books that would be printed in hardcover and shelved in the public library. But he didn't tell his teacher that.

His story was about a kid who wanted to play baseball more than anything in his life. There was a Little League team in the town where he lived and one day at school his friend asked him if he'd like to join. But the kid in the story said no. The truth was he knew his parents couldn't afford the equipment he'd have to buy. They were farmworkers and very poor. He continued to practice, throwing an old softball at a target he'd painted on the door of an abandoned truck, down in a gravel pit on the farm where he and his parents lived. One day the boy's uncle saw him pitching the ball like that and thought he was pretty good. That night he took his nephew aside and gave him a crisp twenty-dollar bill to buy the equipment he needed to join the league.

After he won the prize from the library, and had his picture and his story published in the paper, Ken wondered if maybe he should have told them that the story was mostly true. It was about himself. The only part he'd made up was the piece about the uncle who gave him the twenty-dollar bill. For years he felt guilty about accepting the prize, until he learned that most of the world's great writers also drew their stories from life.

Last year Ken and I met for coffee at a little place on Potrero Hill in San Francisco. We get together about once a year to catch up on each other's lives and talk about writing. I've always looked up to Ken because of his literary accomplishments. When we first met we were both enrolled in the creative writing program at San Francisco State University, and he already had a novel about half done. He was legendary in the department. Before we graduated he'd won two or three prestigious writing grants and an editor at Knopf was negotiating with him for his first book.

About a year after we graduated, he called me one day to say that he'd signed a contract and his novel was coming out in about a year. We were supposed to get together for dinner the following week but he canceled at the last minute. His agent (he now had a literary agent!)

Writers do not live one life, they live two. There is the living and then there is the writing. There is the second tasting, the delayed reaction.

— Anaïs Nin

had been talking with a Hollywood producer who wanted to make a film of his book. They were flying Ken to Spain, where the producer had a summer home, so that they could discuss what Ken's role would be. He was insisting on being the script writer as insurance against the filmmaker straying too far from the original story.

Ken and I didn't get together again for nearly two years. I was alternately jealous and happy for him, awed by his achievement and wondering why I hadn't yet been similarly blessed. In my mind he'd become bigger than life, and I soon developed this strange fear of him that I always have around celebrities. Around friends I bragged that I knew him. But the distance between Ken and me grew until we were nearly strangers.

His book came out and critics heralded him as "the next John Steinbeck." He signed on with the movies, wrote the script, and sat through the entire production, a watchdog protecting his integrity. When the film was released a year later, the critics were generous, calling it "a new American classic."

For a while Ken lived well, yet modestly, off his royalty income. But that was more than twenty-five years ago. He has written only one film script since then, based on a short story he wrote when we were still students. I remembered the story well because I had published it in the small literary quarterly I was editing at the time. I liked the story and I liked the film. But the movie never went anywhere, even though it was good, because the distributors didn't like it. Distributors, Ken explained, will only take films with big-name actors. His film had excellent acting but no big-name actors.

The last time we had coffee, Ken confessed that he hadn't written anything he considered significant since that first novel. He said he didn't even feel inspired any more and asked me how I managed to keep writing. Though I published mostly nonfiction, he said that he liked what I wrote because my books always seemed inspired. He wanted to know where I found that inspiration. How did I keep coming up with it year after year and book after book? I couldn't say just then, but when I got home that night I started thinking more about our conversation.

Ken was one of those people who could tell you the exact moment when he knew he would become a writer. And there's no denying that he had done it. He had one excellent novel and two good film scripts to prove it. But I had to wonder, was that the whole thing? It was as if he loaded his creative cannon at ten, the day he learned that he'd won the short story contest, fired it off at twenty-nine, made some big sparks . . . and that was it. Whatever creative charge drove him to write that one novel was used up in more or less a single shot.

Maybe it's the nature of legends to go out in one big flash like that. Certainly the literary world is replete with such stories. But I have to say that as sadly romantic as they might be, these stories have ceased to interest me except perhaps as warnings.

I can't say I don't feel sorry for Ken and others like him, but I think that I mostly feel impatient, maybe even irritated. If I have literary heroes these days, which I do, they are of a different ilk. Most come from workshops I've taught or from stories people share with me when we talk about writing.

I don't know whether there is a new kind of writer in the world today or if I have just discovered something that has been there all along. I think about Sharon, a retired nun, who signed up for her first writing class at age sixty-seven. Timid and unsure of herself, she read what she claimed was the first short story she'd ever written, dutifully fulfilling the task I'd assigned. In the story, she told about a recent visit to her hometown up in Canada, where she hadn't been since she was a teenager. She went there to look for the house where she'd been born. Instead she found a vacant lot where the family home once stood. There were only waist-high weeds now and a shallow foundation filled with rubble. She described a single sunflower, about six feet tall, with a flower as big as a Cadillac hubcap, standing like a guardian over what had once been the concrete front steps.

Reflecting on that empty lot, Sharon's story took us deep inside her soul, revealing a personal history of pain, hardship, and joy, of early loves and prohibitions, of victories and disappointments, and old wounds that even after sixty years had only begun to heal. In twenty minutes, she took us on a journey into a life that somehow stood for all our lives, showing how human experience lives on in our hearts long after all physical evidence of it has been erased from the earth.

As she finished reading, the room fell silent. When she looked up, it was with an anxious smile, like a child who didn't know what she'd done and was waiting for a sign that would tell her. Across from her, a man in his thirties sat hugging his knees, trying not to cry.

Sharon finally screwed up her courage enough to say, "Well?"

"You'll have to give us all a minute to recover," I said.

"Was it that bad?" she asked.

"No," somebody said. "It was that good!"

Core Concept

Through the artful use of language we build bridges between the consciousness of the author and the consciousness of the reader.

The last time I spoke with Sharon, she was working on a collection of short stories. And if I were a publisher, I can assure you I'd have handed her a contract that day. We talked about writing and I told her again how deeply I'd been touched by that first story she'd read at the workshop.

"I learned a lot that day," she said.

"What, that you are a writer?"

She blushed. "Well, I don't know what it really means to be a writer," she said. "But I did discover how wonderful it is to write. It dissolves boundaries I thought could never be dissolved."

We talked about publishing, and she said, "I don't know as I could ever think of myself as a writer, but one day I'd like to have my work published so that I could go around the country and read my stories to people."

What she said reiterated a truth I've seen expressed many times in writing workshops. It happens at those moments when we forget our literary pretensions and let language do what I have an idea the inventor of the universe intended it to do. Though I don't claim to have any inside track to that entity, I am nevertheless convinced that language was designed to help us bridge one consciousness and another, and to help us connect with that larger consciousness which embraces all and everything.

There's something sad and dangerous about a society that loses touch with this basic understanding, that either puts writing up on a pedestal, or uses it to exploit and manipulate.

I sometimes think that in a past life I must have been the storyteller of a small tribe. When the pressures of publishers' deadlines and arguments with editors start crowding me, I sometimes dream how great it would be to just tell stories to a small circle of friends and neighbors who've gathered around a campfire. And there's no doubt in my mind that we have a lot to learn from those early storytellers, who measured their success by whether or not their stories unveiled previously hidden truths that would improve all their lives, even as they entertained.

Sometimes I think my friend Ken lost sight of what writing is all about. He got seduced by the ivory tower and forgot that being a writer is really something much more than being the literary critics' darling. I don't know what he thought might happen to his life after publishing his novel. Whatever it was he dreamed obviously never came true for him. And the thing that did happen — fame, fortune, kudos from the most respected critics — didn't do it for him.

When language is working for us, the way I think it does for Sharon, it touches something ancient and even primordial and pure in us — if we're open to it happening at all. It's a path into a territory so essential and so elemental that once we're in there we feel like we've come home. It's a place where individual behaviors, different tongues, races, genders, to say nothing of religious and nationalistic identities, cease to divide us. And it's a place where even our harshest self-judgments disappear.

Generally when it happens, it is a fleeting glimpse, as startling as the glowing eyes of a nocturnal creature who dashes off to the side of the road to escape the bright beams of our car's headlights as we race through the night. But as fleeting as these moments might be, they can also change your life forever. They can happen whether you are writing the Great American Novel or an entry in your private journal. These are the moments we yearn to experience in writing, and I'm sure this yearning is the fuel that drives us to put pen to paper.

Rainer Maria Rilke said, "We are only mouth. Who sings the distant heart that dwells entire within all things?" The poet was reflecting on the Logos, the Word, as in St. John's Gospel: "When all things began, the Word already was. The Word dwelt with God, and what God was, the Word was." While I am not a religious scholar by any stretch of the imagination, those opening lines from John's Gospel have always intrigued me, just as they apparently did Rilke.

Some years ago I stumbled upon a book by an obscure but stimulating writer by the name of Georg Kuhlewind, a proponent of Rudolph Steiner's anthroposophy. I really don't know much about anthroposophy or Steiner, but that's not the point. While exploring St. John's writings, Kuhlewind came to believe that the Word "is truly the primal beginning. As soon as something moves, to do something or to think, the Word is there and, with it, the beginning." His point is that since all that moves or thinks came from the Logos (the Word), we are ultimately all joined as one through it. He says, "Without the Logos, there would not be even the attempt to communicate, nor any claim to communication."

Who can say if all this is true or not? I tend to believe that philosophers spend too much time and energy trying to figure things out. Pretty soon they begin to believe themselves and can no longer tell the difference between their own stories and the larger truth they're trying to comprehend. What matters to me in Kuhlewind's speculations is the possibility that language is much more than we think it is. If it's true that all begins with the Word, then maybe what so deeply moves us about writing is that it some-how connects us with our primal source. That spark of recognition and connectedness that we experience when we're really on isn't an illusion. And this drive we feel to write something stunning and glorious isn't self-indulgence or addictive behavior. Rather, what excites us is the recognition that our writing literally builds bridges between our own consciousness, our own life experience, and that of at least one other person. And beyond that we've tapped into that little piece of the Logos we each hold within us, the creative source from which we all come.

There are probably religious leaders who will tell me I'm crazy, or that I'm wrenching the text and treading on dangerous ground. But I don't think so. I believe there is a part of writing that's divine, that connects us with a greater authority than ourselves. And that, certainly, is something we're all born with. If that makes us born writers, so be it. The promise of this is that we can learn to tap into that potential at virtually any point in our lives, trusting that the Word lives in all of us. Whoever dares to claim the prize will have it.

WRITING EXPLORATION #1
DREAM IT TO LIFE

Recall your first experience of creating with the written word. For twenty or thirty minutes, write a short piece about that moment, but write it in the third person, as if you were telling a short story about someone else. Describe the thoughts and feelings you had before, during, and following that first creative writing experience. But remember to tell it in the third person, as if you were looking inside the heart and mind of a man or woman you know extremely well.

OR:

For twenty or thirty minutes write to describe your wildest dreams about how it would be to live as a successful writer. Focus on how you feel about sitting down to write each day, on how you feel upon completion of a book, on how you feel upon the book's publication, and on how you feel when you go out to talk about your writing with groups at bookstores and other meeting places.

CHAPTER TWO

Why We
Must Write

*His [the writer's] function is to make his imagination theirs [the readers']
and he fulfills himself only as he sees his imagination become the light
in the minds of others. His role, in short, is to help people live their lives.*

— Wallace Stevens

Words have always been magical and nourishing for me, perhaps because some of my fondest childhood memories
involve books. Until my older brother and I were about eight years
old, my mother always read to us at bedtime. In those moments
before I slipped off to sleep, vast worlds unfolded in my mind, peopled with marvelous characters, some human, some animal, from
other times and other places. In these imaginative journeys, I
experienced a sense of adventure and wonder. Immersed in those
worlds, I found love and fear, compassion and conflict. The words
formed images that became enchanted paths into the minds and

hearts of people I had never met. And in those moments I began to believe that it might be possible to also share the inner experiences of real people in real life, beyond the pages of books. Life opened up to me through the thoughts, feelings, characters, and places that the stories somehow shaped in my brain. Out of the spectacular make-believe of books, I began to create a vision of what my own life could become.

I was intrigued and thrilled by the worlds those early books opened up to me. At eight or nine years of age, I read my first "big" book, a beautiful thick hardcover of *Treasure Island,* complete with hand-tinted color plates, that my parents gave me for Christmas. By then my mother and father had started a family business and my mother had stopped reading to us in the evenings. She had a small antique and gift shop downtown and would come home at night too tired to carry on the bedtime routine my brother and I had always so deeply enjoyed. But both my parents were also able to communicate to us that, with the family changing, we had to take on more adult responsibilities. Besides, she started bringing home copies of the Hardy Boys mysteries for me to read, which launched me into a reading frenzy that took me through the entire series over the next two or three years.

Television became popular when I was about ten, but until then we had radio, which still depended on the power of language to carry the story. I clearly recall my best friend, Mike, and me lying on the living room floor in front of a giant Philco radio with a huge speaker behind a mahogany grill. Out of that speaker came words and sounds that carried us off into other worlds. Every afternoon, right after school, the two of us listened to the afternoon adventure programs for kids: *Captain Midnight, Batman, The Lone Ranger,* and *Tom Mix.* Here again, words painted pictures in my mind and caused people to come alive in the limitless landscape of my young imagination.

Core Concept

It is not the mere words that excite the creative writer but what words evoke in the human consciousness. The marriage between language and the human spirit is a mystery as ineffable as the spark that fills our hearts when we fall in love.

Today, when I sit down to write, I remember those early years and they remind me of what a miracle language really is. There are times, of course, when in the middle of writing I set my work aside in utter frustration, unable to get the words to do what I am experiencing in my mind. But even at those moments there is still wonder and awe for me in writing, a special pleasure I am certain I will never lose.

Having written for a living most of my adult life, I've done a lot of thinking about language. And I have asked myself many times what so intrigues me about it. There are those who get the same charge out of music or painting pictures on canvas. There are those, like my wife, who find the same delight growing beautiful and exotic flowers. And there are those whose bliss is science, seeking the elusive secrets of the universe.

I know that it is not words per se or the structure of language that intrigues me so much. As any of my teachers would tell you, I have always been pretty indifferent to the rules that govern the way we put words down on paper. More than anything else, it is the marriage between language and the deep mysteries of the human mind that excites me. How is it that with words we can move another person to tears, cause them to laugh, or even communicate a complex scientific principle? Behind the words we find the human consciousness itself — that marvelous instrument without which language would have no meaning.

As lonely and frustrating as the writer's journey can be at times, I can't think of any vocation I'd trade for it. Over the years I've known and worked with literally hundreds of other writers, men and women of all ages who eat, breathe, and dream writing, like addicts addicted to an exotic drug. Every one of them has a story to tell about the thrill of producing their first poem, short story, novel, or essay. And I have seen lives transformed as the dream of becoming an author was transformed into a reality through the publication of a single book.

Not all get famous. Not all get rich — in fact, very few in this business ever do. But there's no denying that our lives take on another dimension when we get into print. I suppose that's one of the most seductive parts of being an author because at that point when we're published, we often discover — sometimes shockingly — the other side of the writing experience. We discover that as intrigued as we might have been by the process of writing itself, an entire new experience is now unfolding. We discover that we are actually being read — not just by our mother or best friend, who adore us and would never say what they really think of our writing, but by thousands of strangers.

I remember my first published book. It was a mystery story, no doubt inspired by my early reading of the Hardy Boys series, for a publisher who specialized in high-interest books for sixth grade through junior high school kids. Writing the story and then working with the editor was a much longer and more arduous task than I could have ever imagined. By the time it was done I was so tired of seeing my own words that I almost didn't care if I ever saw the damned thing again. But the day my editor called to say he had just received a box of books from the printer and I could come over and pick up my ten complimentary copies, my heart battered my inner ribcage with excitement. I raced across town in my car, probably running a couple stoplights in the process and nearly taking the life of a pedestrian. At my publisher's a copy of my first book was pressed into my trembling hands. It was a thin hardcover with a picture of a fishing boat on the cover, depicting the locale where the story took place. I had never known or even thought about the cover art but it was a pleasant surprise, to say the least. I opened the book and pressed it to my face, deeply inhaling the scent of fresh ink on new paper. Then, turning to the first page, I read my words in print for the first time, and in that moment I felt something shift in the way I saw the world and particularly in how I thought about myself. Becoming an author was no longer a fantasy. I had done it! I had really and truly stepped into the life that until then had existed only in my wildest dreams.

I think it took me nearly a year to get used to thinking of myself as an author. To tell you the truth, I still have trouble with that from time to time, even after publishing numerous books. But there was no denying the wonderful, if daunting, truth. I could hold the book in my hand, or occasionally read a page or two from it, and feel a certain thrill and sense of accomplishment that I'd never before enjoyed. But it was not until I was asked one day to read from it as part of a library program for young people that I grasped the full significance of being a published author.

I was terribly nervous the day of that reading. All sorts of fantasies ran through my head. Most of them were pretty disturbing, such as the voice that said to me, "You're not a real author! Who do you think you are getting up and pretending such a thing in front of a bunch of kids?" I think this came from very old conditioning in my past, when both my parents and teachers told me that I was not much of a student and should probably seek employment as a factory worker or salesman. But on the appointed morning of the reading, still steeped in self-doubt, I faced a roomful of children in a musty room in the big downtown San Francisco

Public Library and heard the librarian introducing me, telling about the exciting story I had written and that I would be reading it to them that day.

With voice quavering and knees shaking behind the podium, I began reading, careful not to look up from the page for fear of seeing their faces and losing my nerve. Five minutes into the story, however, I noticed that the room had become deathly quiet. Screwing up my courage, I put my finger on the page so that I wouldn't lose my place, then looked up. What I saw amazed me. All eyes were on me, faces intent, some with jaws dropped open in awe. I realized then that they were completely caught up in my story.

It took me about forty-five minutes to read the book, editing out two or three parts where the action bogged down a little. Afterwards, hands shot up from the crowd of young listeners, asking what happened to this character or that afterwards. Was the main character's mother scared when the teenaged hero was kidnapped for two days? When he grew up, did he get a boat and become a fisherman like his father?

I realized that my budding young readers had been completely convinced that the world I had created was real. To them these people I'd shaped from my fantasies were as real as their best friends or family members. They cared about them and wanted to know more about their lives. I tried to explain that all this was fiction, but somehow they didn't seem convinced. Through my words I had created a world of people and situations that mattered to them as much as their own daily lives.

I came away from that reading with a very different perspective about my writing. Beyond the thrill of publishing my first book, there was the realization that what we create with our words can have a very real impact on other people's lives. It is as if through our words, we enter their minds. We mingle our own inner worlds with our readers', in many cases touching their lives in ways that will change them forever.

Despite my early success writing children's stories, it quickly became clear to me that if I was to survive economically in the world of publishing I'd better turn to nonfiction. In any case, I never had any great illusions about writing the Great American Novel or a philosophical treatise that would revolutionize human thought. Within the next five years, writing only at night after work, I completed and had three more books published, two of them fiction and one nonfiction. Then, following a motorcycle accident that hospitalized me for two months, I became obsessed with the idea of writing a popular medical book. While in the hospital I'd noticed that people who were injured or ill seemed to surrender all their

I write entirely to find out what I'm thinking, what I'm looking at, what I see and what it means. What I want and what I fear.

— Joan Didion

power, and their responsibility for their health, over to their physicians. Part of the problem, it seemed to me, was that people didn't even know enough about their own bodies or medicine to ask intelligent questions.

After recovering from the accident, I began looking for a doctor with whom to write a book that would empower people to take charge of their own health. This was in the late 1960s, long before there was the standard health section now found in most bookstores. At the time the health book selection in most stores was limited to two books: *The Red Cross First Aid Manual* and a huge, forbidding hardcover called *The Better Homes and Garden Home Medical Encyclopedia*. Most publishers thought my idea crazy, as did most doctors I talked to as potential collaborators.

Then, in 1970, I met Mike Samuels, a doctor who also believed that there was a real need for a friendly book that would give people the information they needed to take greater responsibility for their own health. The book would challenge some sacred cows and traditions that had been upheld in our culture for nearly a century, but our main goal was to demystify personal health and build a new model for wellness. We found a publisher, wrote it in nine months — originally, a seven-hundred-page manuscript! — nearly destroying our own health in the process. Within a year and a half from the beginning of the project, we had finished books rolling into the stores. It was a big, oversized yellow book with a colorful hand-rendered caduceus on the cover. We called it *The Well Body Book*. Unbeknownst to us at the time it would prove, in the next couple of years, to be a pivotal book, initiating a brand-new genre of books and supporting a revolutionary way of thinking about our own bodies.

When that book first came out, we toured colleges and bookstores throughout the West, talking about our concepts, and even demonstrating how people could take their own blood pressure, test their own urine, and do their own pelvic exams. We taught relaxation techniques, discussed the role of physical exercise and health, and even ways to diagnose and treat common diseases. At many of our lectures there was invariably an old-line medical professional who attacked what we were doing, reciting the old homily that "a little knowledge about such complex and critical issues as medicine could be dangerous." To such criticisms we always replied by quoting T. H. Huxley, who said, "If a little knowledge is dangerous, where is the man who has so much as to be out of danger?"

In spite of our critics, our efforts spurred the imagination of a whole generation, giving impetus to the wellness movement we take so much for granted today. Less than five years following its debut, doctors were ordering *The Well Body Book* for their waiting rooms, and in many cases physicians were prescribing the books to their patients. In less than ten years, it was being published in seven languages, selling a grand total of nearly a quarter million copies.

As an author, I learned numerous lessons in that experience. The primary one was that when my coauthor, Mike Samuels, and I sat down to write that book we had no idea it would have such a powerful social impact. Moreover, there was something almost otherworldly about how the book was conceived. Many parts seemed to come from sources outside us, as if there were an invisible coach telling us what the world wanted at that time. If the truth must be known, we have both had trouble taking much credit for that book. We have always been aware that we were riding a wave that involved probably thousands of people, some of them ordinary people seeking a better way of caring for their own health, others being doctors who knew there was something wrong about the high priest system that dominated modern medicine at that time. Mike and I were carried along on a wave far bigger than either of us, or both of us together, as it were. One thing is undeniable — that the book made a big difference in people's lives, and that we were privileged to be perhaps the equivalent of two tiny cells in the awakening of a new consciousness about personal health.

C o r e   C o n c e p t

As writers, we do not always know what forces are acting upon us, guiding us to write this or that. When the call comes, maybe we shouldn't question its source but trust and follow its lead.

As a budding young author, I was mystified. This book had come out of a completely unexpected experience. What could be more unexpected, or at least unplanned, than a traffic accident! Yet, out of that ordeal my passion for writing this book was born. During college I read about the legendary muse that awakened the passions of poets. But if this was the sort of stimulus I required to write, I decided I'd better start looking for another line of work.

Over the years, I have worked with literally hundreds of authors, some of them celebrities in their fields, others ordinary people with something they felt was important to say. In the process, I've become as intrigued by the creative chemistry of the writer as I am with the act of writing itself. I find myself asking questions, such as, What are the deep inner resources from which successful authors draw? How do authors connect with that passion, bordering on obsession, that drives them to finish even the most ambitious writing projects in spite of seemingly insurmountable handicaps? How do we tap into and express the joys, sorrows, hopes, and fears that prod our readers to action or move them emotionally? What is the secret creative energy the world's best writers can apparently zap into action the moment their fingers touch the keyboard of their word processors? And what is it about the special bond between author and reader that makes writing so seductive, tempting, and irresistible? I believe there are answers to these questions, some of them quite surprising, though I believe there are some essential secrets about language and writing that the universe will never disclose to us.

Not all the gifted writers I've had the privilege of knowing have been published. Many are not even interested in doing so. Instead, they are members of a fast-growing fellowship who consider private writing in journals to be an essential part of their spiritual and personal development. I have grown to have increasing respect for these men and women who, maybe even more than those of us interested in publishing, have discovered the real power of language as a vehicle to explore the inner space of human consciousness.

I have been truly blessed to witness those extraordinary breakthrough moments in people's lives when through their own creativity they come into their power as writers. Time and time again, I have sat spellbound as a person read lines from a short story, poem, essay, or journal entry they had written, watching the faces of the others as their hearts and minds, their very souls, were moved by the words. Though similarly moved by the words, I am frequently awed by something more, something the person reading may not yet know — that this breakthrough experience will change their life forever.

If you do not breathe through writing, if you do not cry out in writing, or sing in writing, then don't write, because our culture has no use for it.

— Anaïs Nin

My approach to writing, I'm afraid, has never been particularly literary. I have an idea this may have started as a reaction to graduating from a college creative writing program, where Literature with a capital "L" was elevated on a golden pedestal, high up in the proverbial Ivory Tower. I always had the feeling that we were supposed to worship rather than to have our lives transformed by the writings of people like Joseph Conrad, Dostoyevsky, and even — yes, they definitely would have said "even" — John Steinbeck, who my teachers considered little more than a journalist with literary pretensions.

There was always the not-so-hidden message that high literature should be the goal of every graduate of the program, though try as we might we would probably never make it. Being far more proletarian than that, in my tastes as well as in my experiences as a reader, I constantly rebelled. In protest to one teacher's particularly stuffy approach to literature, I handed in a love story I'd written, about half of which consisted of a very graphic sex scene. I received a C-minus for my efforts, with a note scrawled in red pencil at the top: "We are not here to encourage young pornographers! Try to keep your literary efforts to a higher standard." I framed that page with its indignant scrawl at the top and hung it on the wall behind my desk. It was a message to me that I should stick to a truth I'd first experienced as a child — that the real value of words for me was found in the delight of worlds they awakened in my own consciousness, not in blind adoration or literary scholarship.

There are moments in all our lives so poignant, funny, tender, or perhaps even violent and heartbreaking that communicating them well transports both writer and reader out of their everyday view of the world, expanding their experience of life. Even more than the great literary works, I remember scenes by my own students. I recall the delicately drawn journal entry written by a young woman, telling of her first-time love, of a fumbling young man she loved very deeply but in her own clumsiness didn't know how to comfort and reassure when he couldn't consummate their passion. In this case, it was a true story about losing what is most precious in our lives because of the sheer bewilderment and embarrassment of our innocence. And I also remember the man — a cop with a poet's sensitivity — who read us a scene from his novel-in-progress, describing an actual event he had witnessed during his years in Vietnam, when his best friend went berserk and opened fire on a mountain village, slaughtering dozens of women and children and turning what had been a pastoral rural setting into a bloody holocaust.

When the writer tells it from her or his soul, even the most gruesome or embarrassing or uplifting or unconscionable or even puzzling experiences can bring us closer, can remind us of our own humanness and help us more deeply appreciate the gift of life. I tend to agree with Wallace Stevens, whose words I used at the beginning of this chapter, when he said that our role as writers is to help people — including ourselves, I would add — live their lives. I do believe that we fulfill ourselves when we can see our creations become the light in the minds of others. What do we need to know to accomplish this? Unfortunately, there's no simple answer. But the purpose of this book is to explore how to do that, to see and feel and hear and even taste what it's like when writers achieve it.

Language is one of those God-given gifts that we often take so much for granted. We speak of people having good or poor communication skills, or we see language only as a way of conveying information. But I think it's much more than that. Perhaps there is a power greater than ourselves that gave it to us so that we might build bridges between our consciousnesses, allowing us to transcend the sense of separation we experience most of the time and so step, if only for brief instants, into our essential Oneness. Through words well crafted, like a superb bowl found in an archaeological dig, we provide evidence for the invisible inner worlds that make each of our lives unique, while also touching that ultimate point we all share with our hearts, making each strongly felt experience universal.

Through my own writing, through the dozens of other writers with whom I've had the opportunity to work, and through the students who have taught me so much over the years, I feel as if I've become the custodian of certain insights about what makes good writing work. In the final analysis, I believe that what this book offers is not techniques but a kind of cartography, mapping out the relatively unknown territory of the writer's mind. For whatever they're worth, I offer them with a word of caution: Taking this information to heart, and really applying it in your writing, can and will change your life.

If you take your journey as a writer seriously, the end product is going to be much more than a published book, poem, article, story, or a lifetime of personal journals. The path will take you beyond the surface of everyday life, toward the inner space of human experience, where you cannot escape the awareness of creative sources far greater than any single one of us. You will discover, somewhere in infinitude of that seemingly private universe, heavenly bodies that every one of us sees if we have the courage to look. When we're at our most impactful as writers, those bright stars of inner space shine through, inspiring awe and uplifting our hearts.

Even while extolling the powers of language in this way, I want to be careful I don't give the impression that our goal is to produce only "high literature." I doubt that anyone sets out to do that anyway. The greatness, if it does come across, comes because the author writes from his or her soul; it doesn't happen under the pretense of trying to impress the scholars. I have found as many uplifting and awe-inspiring passages in private journals as I have in the "great works" of the acknowledged masters. Similarly, being an avid mystery reader, I have met characters and situations from such entertainments that have moved and even enlightened me as deeply as anything in Great Literature.

Core Concept

The act of writing is not as solitary as one might think. When it finally dawns on us one day that our task as writers is to share what we know of the human spirit, we suddenly discover that we were never truly alone. If we write without this awareness, our words never come to life on the page, and we might better be working for The Corporation, where anonymity is better valued and the rewards more easily counted.

Rather, writing is a spiritual act because it invites us to look beyond the surface of life, to attempt to capture the essence of love, grief, joy, fear, compassion, pride, forgiveness, nobility, wretchedness — in short, the whole gamut of human existence. To write well we have to open up to ourselves and to others. And as we'll be exploring in later chapters, language by its very nature does this, implying a sharing, an interchange between individuals that breaks through the barriers of our separateness. Why else invest all the energy that goes into learning to speak or write?

Without language, we live in relative isolation, cut off from others of our own species. That was the biblical lesson in the story of the Tower of Babel, wherein the people of Shinar, who once spoke a single language and had much power, attempted to build a tower with its top in heaven, so that they might themselves be as gods and gain control of the entire world. To discourage their efforts, God confused their speech so that they would not understand one another. Without their common language their strength was negated because they could no longer coordinate their efforts to finish the tower.

Through the laws of language, we literally dissolve the distance between ourselves. We discover and share with others the uniqueness of our own life experience, and in doing so we discover the spiritual source that bonds us one to another.

Presumably, we will not be punished for this — though one might be advised against challenging God's superiority by building a tower to reach the heavens!

WRITING EXPLORATION #2
TRUST YOUR PASSION

Have you ever stopped to think about the passion that drives you as a writer? For the moment, put all thoughts of commercial success aside. Drop your thoughts about the fulfillment of dreams you may have about writing, and forget all thoughts about the difficulties of getting published or otherwise recognized for your writing. Instead, just get in touch with the single idea, or group of ideas, that you feel passionate about expressing. Let what is in your heart speak rather than getting into arguments with yourself about whether or not publishers or anyone else would go for it. Give your passions the reins. Then spend some time thinking about how you would want readers to be affected by what you have expressed. How would you like your readers to be moved? What actions would you like them to take as a result of what you have written? Or, simply, what state of mind would you want them to be experiencing after reading your work?

CHAPTER THREE

A Place of Your Own

That inward eye

Which is the bliss of solitude.

— William Wordsworth

E arly one morning, a day before my forty-second birthday, I put a change of clothes and a few extras into my backpack, lashing that, a small tent, and a sleeping bag onto the back of my motorcycle. Saying goodbye to my family, and promising to be back in four days, I set out for the Gold Country, a hundred and fifty miles east of my home.

As evening approached I stopped to make camp at Calaveras Big Trees, in a canyon they call Squaw Hollow, three miles back off Highway 4. Eating tuna from a can, I lounged at the timber-heavy picnic table near my tent and realized I was probably one of the last campers of the season, at least until the deer hunters came later that month, skulking into the woods with their guns.

I could smell rain in the distance, the sky heavy, clouds iron gray, a chilling breeze. But I felt okay about the weather, slept well, and dreamed. Just before dawn I was awakened by a small black bear blundering into the guy-line of my tent. Sticking my head out between the flaps of my mosquito netting door, the bear and I stared eye to eye for a second, her long nose black and shiny, close enough for me to smell her fetid breath. Then she fled, the fat under her shaggy black fur wobbling on her haunches, attesting to the fact that she had prepared herself well for winter, probably plumping herself up on stale doughnuts and watermelon rinds from garbage cans spilling over from tourists' refuse.

Late the next afternoon, I climbed to a ridge high above my camp; Thunder Hill to the north and McKee Hill further east rose like magnificent grassy knolls, their rippling terrain carpeted with forests of spruce and fir, the skies clear. For two or three hours I climbed, exploring trails clogged with underbrush, barely passable. I moved cautiously, conscious of my path, avoiding fragile plants, wildflowers, passing a pair of grazing deer, two does, who only raised their heads briefly and stared, chewing, a little annoyed by my intrusion.

I'd brought a camera along, and against the backdrop of dense forests I stopped to take pictures of a gray squirrel hunting nuts in the tall, dry weeds. The reddening evening light cast a smooth patina along golden stalks, the squirrel more silver than gray now, alert, tail curling up along its back, head erect and swiveling, scanning the earth in short, quick jerks, searching for me, smelling danger. Undiscovered, I lay on my stomach, squinting through the viewfinder of my Japanese camera, proud of my craftiness, glad to go unnoticed. The squirrel gave up his fear. Through my camera's eye, a single weed, slender, golden, waving, bowed against the breeze, etched the sky, rare, alone, heavy with seeds.

Still later, having hiked further on, I stood atop another ridge and watched the sun vanish, the glow over the forest soft and flat. For a while I saw seven horizons, seven receding planes of hills and trees, one behind another, like a stage set for a play. And because the sun was gone, the horizon had begun to turn gray, a black-and-white photo. The camera jiggled as I snapped the shutter.

They say that in the dark we see only in black and white, something to do with the nature of our eyes. So, imagining green more than seeing it, I felt an urge to return to my camp, maybe fearing the loss of color, a primal mystery reborn each night. In the distance I found the top of my tent through a clearing in the trees, its light blue geometry now gray, a few feet away the picnic table, black now, and the motorcycle leaning on its kickstand, crisp, man-made, a foreigner in this ageless environment.

My camp looked comfortable, neat, inviting me. It felt good seeing it in the distance, through the trees, and for a while I sat on the hill and enjoyed what I felt, seeing it. The world took my silence for indifference, and in moments the treetops above me came alive. Squirrels worked the branches, pulling pinecones and breaking them apart for their nuts, then letting go, the cones crashing down through the solemn hearts of the trees, soft and final thuds signaling their arrival on earth.

Back at camp the mosquitoes were thick. I made a small fire in the circle of stones near my tent, the scent and smoke of the burning pine logs driving off the buzzing pests. Not wanting to cook, I sliced open a ripe avocado I bought at the store the day before and ate it with a spoon. There was also a small chunk of cheddar cheese from Sonoma, some nuts and raisins, and a small bottle of Cabernet that I'd cooled under some rocks in the river fifty yards from camp. I ate slowly, sipping the wine, getting up when the mosquitoes started up again to put another log on the fire.

By the time I'd finished eating, it was dark and already growing cold. I lit a small candle lantern and set it on the table, wanting to write. I could see my breath in the air. The moon, bright, marbled the earth with shadows as it filtered down through the branches sheltering my camp. I shivered, writing in my small notebook, finally got up and put on my riding jacket, then shivered more as I zippered it closed, the cool leather at first ungiving. But in a few moments, the heat from my own body, closed inside, warmed me and the protective leather felt secure and known, molding to my body in the way it had done for more than a dozen years.

I sat and wrote for over an hour, and thought there could be nothing better than to sit and write, alone in the darkness at a table in the forest. Late, maybe ten o'clock, I boiled some water at my campfire and made a cup of tea. I'd finished writing by then and had an urge for a cigarette or maybe a pipe of tobacco, though I hadn't smoked in years.

I heard footsteps on the gravel road that passed a few yards north of my campsite, then heard voices, a late-night conversation of two people who'd grown old together and knew what it took to gentle each other. I do not know where their camp was. I hadn't seen any-one else come in during the day, but there they were in the moonlight. Their voices came to me abstracted, sounds that told me more than words. I couldn't see their faces in the forest shadows but saw white hair and slender, straight, strong aging bodies that I was certain still embraced each other's youth. They passed and I was alone again, content.

The trees became bold black lines against the sky, silvered by a bright round moon and the Milky Way. Crickets chirped vaguely, their songs discouraged by the cold, replacing the day's last color with sound.

When I write stories I am like someone who is in her own country, walking along streets that she has known since she was a child, between walls and trees that are hers.

— Natalia Ginsburg

Fifteen years later, I still call upon the memory of this and other periods of delicious solitude when the world around me seems too busy or demanding, resisting the peace the writer in me needs. I am not sure what it is in me that demands those slightly sad but settled and centered feelings that come with solitude, but whatever that state of mind is, it's a tremendously important part of the whole process. I find it impossible to write with another person in the room, and it's just as difficult for me to write outside, unless under the protection of towering trees or the darkness.

I am always amazed when people tell me their favorite place to write is in a café or a public library. I remember one time walking into a small café in Santa Fe and noticing a young woman sitting alone at one of those tiny round tables, hardly big enough to hold her notebook, a paperback dictionary she'd brought along, and her café latte. In addition, K.D. Lang was singing "Constant Craving" in the background, and a thin blond man with a bright yellow T-shirt advertising Corona beer was shrieking into the receiver of the pay phone, letting the world know that he was enraged about somebody named Chris who had failed to show up for a date.

If you are a writer you locate yourself behind a wall of silence and no matter what you are doing, driving a car or walking or doing housework . . . you can still be writing, because you have that space.

— Joyce Carol Oates

The woman writing at the table kept her head down and her pen moving, apparently oblivious to what was happening all around her. For all I know, this was where she found her solitude, alone in a café, surrounded by strangers.

I'm not sure I've always recognized the importance of putting myself into that state of mind but it is very clear to me at this point in my life that it is essential to the creative process. Probably the first time I really became aware of the power of such moments was under the giant redwoods in Kings Canyon, at the southern entrance to Yosemite. I had driven up from Ventura, where I lived at the time, and had rented a small cabin for the week. With no electricity I wrote by the light of a kerosene lamp placed on a crude plank table. I put my words down on the lined yellow paper of a legal pad, using my favorite fountain pen, a maroon Esterbrook with a gold-tipped nib that I found in a secondhand store in Santa Barbara. The silence and the darkness under the trees were profound. Acutely aware of my senses, in that natural sensory deprivation chamber, I wrote, "Nature is where there is no voice but the one you put there." The inner world from which I drew creative inspiration seemed to have been turned up a thousand decibels with only the scent of redwood and molding leaves competing for my attention.

Many years later, while my family was still young, it became virtually impossible for me to find the kind of solitude I needed in the house. I rented an office in town for a while, in a small building in the warehouse district of Berkeley. But it didn't work. There was privacy but there was also a constant buzzing of activity, of trucks going by, of the air conditioner humming, of phones ringing in other offices around me and above me. I certainly felt isolated and alone, but this was definitely not solitude.

One night I had a dream of writing in this very small house at the back of a wild, unkempt garden. From the outside, it looked like nothing more than a toolshed or a potting shed, but once inside there were bookshelves from floor to ceiling, a built-in L-shaped desk that took up most of the floor space, a tiny sleeping loft, and under the desk rows and rows of drawers. From a mahogany swivel chair in the center of the room, virtually every drawer and bookshelf was within arm's reach. Two dormer windows looked out over tangles of wild roses, a profusion of subtle reds, pinks, and yellows, providing an illusion of space that was quite surprising. Inside, the entire space glowed with the warmth of dark, hand-finished wood. Outside, there were the roses, a small apple tree further on, and beyond that a flowering plum, resplendent with its outrageous pink blossoms.

When I woke up the next morning I walked into our backyard and saw where the tiny building should go. The rest — the trees and flowers — were pretty much in place. With a friend's help I built the structure in about two weeks, moved in my writing materials and books, and before the month came to an end was happily composing my next manuscript.

This was without a doubt the most perfect writing space I had ever had. It contained me, like a womb, and in the security of those walls, with everything I needed at arm's length, my consciousness was free to roam. I wrote several books there over the next five years. When I moved on, that was the thing I missed most.

However you define it, and however you get it, every writer needs a place of solitude. I always have to remind myself, however, that it is a state of mind, not a place. Once we know what it is, what it looks like and feels like, we can create it for ourselves, almost — I say *almost* — regardless of where we happen to be. All writers discover how to get it for themselves, in time. For Hemingway, it was Paris, apparently the entire city, and once he had experienced it he had it for life. He said, "If you are lucky enough to have lived in Paris as a young man, then wherever you go for the rest of your life, it stays with you, for Paris is a movable feast."

If the solitude writers yearn for comes in different packages, I also believe that it has some fairly universal characteristics. The most important one, I would think, is a certain sense of safety, not safety from physical danger, such as getting struck by lightning or being abducted by space aliens, so much as a guarantee against insensitive interruptions. The creative process requires that we leave the external world and go into the inner one. And while in that inner one, we don't want to be reminded of the external one. A telephone ringing, a spouse rushing into the room in search of the car keys, a child shrieking in your ear, demanding your attention — all these jerk you out of that inner world that is the life force of the writer. These are not just simple interruptions; to the person thoroughly immersed in the work of writing, they are assaults. Solitude nurtures us, respects the process that we need to follow if we're to fulfill our dream.

Core Concept

What the writer calls solitude is not a mood or sentiment so much as it is permission to journey inward to the most private place of all, an inner world where we might find a nourishing seascape, or perhaps walk through serene villages or urban neighborhoods heaving with life, where we feel a quiet contentment.

I used to believe that this nurturing place of safety we call solitude was an easy and natural thing, that everyone knew what it was and experienced it in their lives at least once in a while. Then, several years ago, I was asked by my friend Gabrielle Roth to address a large workshop group she was teaching in northern California. There were about seventy people, and I was to spend three hours with each of four smaller segments of the larger group. But as an introduction I was to walk them through a guided visualization exercise I have for creating a safe writing place, a place of solitude, an inner writing studio.

Halfway through the exercise, somebody started sobbing. Then another person joined in, then another. When we'd completed the guided imagery portion of the exercise, I asked people to share with us what their places of solitude looked like and felt like. To my amazement, many people described these places with tears in their eyes, and even with much sobbing and grief. One woman in her early forties said that as I guided them through the exercise she suddenly realized that she had never in her life had a space of her own. As a child, she had shared a bedroom with her sister. In college she had roommates. While still in college, she married and then shared her bedroom with her husband. She also realized that between raising her children, having a part-time job, and trying to be a good wife, she was rarely alone. The closest thing to solitude she'd ever enjoyed was in the bathroom taking a shower. Through the guided imagery exercise, she created an imaginary place of solitude, what she called her "magical garden," where she could sit and meditate for hours or simply lie naked in the sun while butterflies and hummingbirds fluttered about.

She was not alone. At least a half-dozen others in the class shared the same mixture of sadness and joy at discovering the lack of solitude in their lives — sadness because they had gotten in touch with something profound and rich that was missing from their lives, and joy because they had at last gotten in touch with what they'd been missing. The men in the class reported fewer problems with solitude. Most of them had not only experienced it many times, they almost took it for granted, demanding and getting it from the world. Men reported experiencing it in sports, while running alone on a favorite trail, while working in a home workshop, while fishing, or even while driving to work in the mornings.

The people who dream of writing but can't, who complain of "writer's block," or of simply being unable to begin, are the same ones who have no place of solitude in their lives. There's not a doubt in my mind that this is where good writing begins. I'm not saying it has to be in a rustic cabin under the redwoods or at a romantic café in Paris. But without some place to go, either in our minds or in our physical lives, where we can feel the luxury of solitude, the writer in you can never come out. I'm sure this is the place Wordsworth was talking about when he spoke of the "inward eye which is the bliss of solitude."

WRITING EXPLORATION #3
CREATE YOUR IDEAL WRITING SPACE

I used to do this long, meditative exercise for my classes, starting out with a deep relaxation technique, and then guiding people step by step into mental imagery of an ideal writing place. And then I remembered that good writing takes us there. That's what it's all about. So the ideal situation would be to give our writing this double purpose — taking us into the solitude, the ideal writing place, while also actually getting some writing practice. The assignment turns out to be one of those pulling-yourself-up-by-your-own-bootstraps sort of things. The writing puts you where you need to be to start writing, and you've actually started writing in the process.

One way to do this is to work from memory. Go as far back as you want or need to get hold of your solitude. Or maybe you've had a relatively recent experience of solitude you'd like to work with. It might be a fleeting moment. The best example that comes to mind of this was something a woman did in a workshop I gave in Ashland, Oregon. She was a runner and some of her best but most fleeting moments of solitude came during her morning runs on this particular road out in the hills. So she wrote about that. She wrote about the steep grade and the narrow, winding blacktop road and the big dog at the beginning of the run that always charged against its chain in the front yard of this farmer's house and frightened her at the start of her run. It was a big black dog with a wide, thick jaw, and she was always afraid that one day it would break its chain, come after her, and tear her to pieces. But it never did, and every time she ran it was the same thing. A half-mile past the dog, the road leveled out and she found her pace and it felt wonderful running on the dirt shoulder alongside the road, which was softer than the blacktop.

It was, of course, impossible to imagine how she could run and write, too. But she said that after a mile or so the running became automatic and she started writing in her mind. In her mind, she was sometimes a million miles away, in faraway places she had visited or dreamed of visiting. She'd make up poems, and when she got back to her apartment in town she wrote down what she remembered. She said it was always the solitude of the run that got her into that place where her creativity took flight. Afterward, it was like taking dictation to get the words down because she had a very good memory, almost as good as having a tape recorder along.

If you can't recall moments of solitude, make them up. Where would you like to be? If you could have any writing studio you wanted, what would it look like? One man told about a beautiful cottage that clung to the side of the cliff overlooking the rocky coast around Big Sur, south of Carmel, California. Waves crashed under it, sending showers of seawater against the windows. In this imaginary writing place he had a servant who brought him his meals, always perfectly prepared gourmet food, and a masseuse who arrived every afternoon to give him a massage so that his shoulders didn't cramp up from sitting all morning at the word processor. Everyone in the class loved the fantasy, though none of us ever knew a writer who could afford that kind of luxury in real life. It didn't matter because the point is that you only need to have it in your own mind. In your mind you can have anything in the world you'll allow yourself to have. There are no limits.

Write your description of this place of solitude with plenty of sensory clues thrown in. Describe what you see: specific colors (the blue sky, the golden summer hills); smells (seaweed rotting in the sun); touch (sinking into the soft leather chair); temperature (shivering as I leaned over and touched a match to the neat little tepee of paper and kindling wood I'd set up in the fireplace); sounds (a gentle breeze rustling the leaves of the oaks outside my window, the crickets chirping); and mood (my sadness at her parting slips away and I suddenly feel strangely elated). Remember that the point is to put yourself into the scene. It's through describing what we perceive through our senses that gets us there and takes the reader with us. It's not a bad idea, in fact, to make a list of the five senses and put it on the wall above your desk: sight, sound, touch, taste, and smell. Add emotion to that if you wish, but when you write, always concentrate on what triggers those emotions, describing these triggers in terms of the senses.

If you have a good friend you can read to, do that when you've finished your description. If your writing carries them along with you, into your place of solitude, you'll know you've succeeded. Having the experience of reading your own writing to another person is tremendously important; we don't complete our writing until we've done that. Wherever we use language, there's an implied reader. Even people like Emily Dickinson, famous for spiriting her poems away in a drawer so people wouldn't read them, knew that. She wrote:

> *A word is dead*
> *When it is said,*
> *Some say.*
> *I say it just*
> *Begins to live*
> *That day.*

Once you've written about your solitude and the place you associate with it, use it whenever you sit down to write. Remember that your greatest power as a writer, what you draw from for your inspiration, isn't out there but inside you. I like to quote this great line from Alfred North Whitehead: "The poets are entirely mistaken. They should address their lyrics to themselves, and should turn them into odes of self-congratulation on the excellency of the human mind. Nature is a dull affair, soundless, scentless, colorless; merely the hurrying of material, endlessly, meaninglessly."

It's not easy to remember that we are always, quite literally, making sense of our world. Nature doesn't have the scent of a rose; we make it up with the raw data we get from our senses, and then we mix it together with all sorts of associations that are stored in our brains. At best it's a kind of conspiracy between ourselves and what's out there, since we are, after all, as much creations of nature as are the roses. I know that when I can remember that we are always projecting meaning onto whatever is happening out there, and that there's really not much else any of us can do, it makes my work as a writer a little easier. Most of all, it reminds me that the most important and generous thing any of us has to give as an author is our own voice, how we each experience our lives.

Maybe it's only in solitude that we can hear that voice clearly. And maybe that's as true for our readers as it is for ourselves.

CHAPTER FOUR

Is Anybody Out There?

'Tis the good reader that makes the good book;
in every book he finds passages which seem confidences or asides
hidden from all else and unmistakably meant for his ear;
the profit of books is according to the sensibility of the reader;
the profoundest thought or passage sleeps as in a mine,
until it is discovered by an equal mind and heart.

— Ralph Waldo Emerson

The first successful nonfiction book I wrote was one about home schooling and setting up small private schools as an alternative to public education. The book came out of firsthand experiences, when my own family and friends started sending our kids off to public schools. I discovered that far more parents than I would ever have dreamed were dissatisfied or just plain angry at the way their kids were being treated in school, but they did not know what to do instead.

In an effort to find some solutions, I started collecting information about taking our kids out of public schools and starting schooling programs in our homes. I wrote a fifty-page booklet on it and sold it for a couple of dollars through ads in the classified sections of rebel newspapers around San Francisco and Berkeley. I didn't sell a lot of them, but one day an editor from a small publishing company called up and asked me a lot of questions about it. I told him all I knew, and then he said he'd like to talk with me about doing a whole book on it.

His name was Don Gerrard. In the mid-1960s, before starting his own publishing company that would later become a Random House imprint, he was a book rep for one of the major publishers. He traveled all around northern California visiting bookstores and filling orders for the newest books. In his travels, he began to see a growing number of people publishing books and magazines out of their garages or kitchens, people doing some very exciting new work that the larger New York publishers didn't yet understand. Many of these publishing ventures were extremely successful, catering to that growing number of young men and women who were discontented with the way things were and wanted to make some changes. They were making changes by literally creating their own society inside the larger one.

Don Gerrard had the foresight to recognize this as something more than a passing fad. That's the way most East Coast publishers were choosing to look at it, meanwhile missing literally millions of dollars worth of book sales each year. New York editors looked at the books published "out West" and invented a new term, "nonbooks," presumably because most of them were how-to books.

The problem was distribution; these alternative publishers could get their material written, printed, and bound, but they had only limited channels for getting their products to their readers. Don took on several small publishers, peddling their wares out of the trunk of his car, while continuing to sell his regular line of New York–style books.

The business in alternative books grew at an astronomical rate. Seeing the writing on the wall, Don started one of the first successful independent book distributors, called Bookpeople, which continues to be a strong and influential force in the book world today. After that, Don started Bookworks, a publishing company of his own.

Don set up an evening appointment with me, because I had a teaching job at the time, and gave me an address in a rather seedy warehouse district of Berkeley where we were to meet. I found a heavy metal door with the number he'd given me stenciled on it. I knocked and after several minutes, Don answered. He led me into a well-lit office with an Oriental carpet on the floor, a large wooden rocking chair, a big leather couch, and a bookshelf I later learned held copies of every independently published book he'd ever represented.

Don was in his early thirties then, a tall, good-looking man with a scruffy beard and a hint of a Texas accent. He apologized for not being able to offer me tea or a cup of coffee. He explained something about a small kitchen in the hallway between his and the adjoining office but the door into it was locked at night.

He sat opposite me in the rocking chair while I lounged back on the couch, separated by a coffee table made of a huge redwood burl that supported an oval plate-glass top. He had brought along a manila folder containing some notes he'd made about my prospective book. He flipped through his papers for a moment, then looked up at the ceiling.

"Who do you think is your reader? Could you describe them?"

His question caught me off guard. I shrugged. "I suppose people like me, people who've had their kids in public school and maybe had a bad experience with it."

He nodded. "Your writing's okay. It's clear. You get the information down and all that but then it doesn't go any place."

"It hopefully gets read," I answered, somewhat defensively. I really didn't get what he was driving at.

"Don't get me wrong," he said, apparently eager to keep me on his side. "I like what you're doing here. But when I sit down to read a book for myself, I look for certain things that I guess a lot of other people don't. And for better or for worse, that's what I try to publish. I like to publish books I want to read.

"I'm not necessarily talking about content," he said. "It's more a way of writing I'm looking for."

"A certain style, then?"

"I'm not sure I'd call it style. It's more an attitude, a way the writer has of acknowledging me, the reader."

I pondered this for a moment. "But that would require me to actually be there, to know the reader."

"In a sense, yes. I can't tell you how to do it, since I'm not a writer. But I know it when I see it, and I can tell you this much, it has partly to do with using personal pronouns — I, me, and you, mostly."

Don gave me some photocopied samples of writing that he liked, gleaned from several different books. He told me to go home, look over the papers he'd handed me, and try to write three or four pages as if I was writing a letter to a very good friend, covering the same material. He said that after he'd seen what I could do, we'd talk about the rest of the book and about his publishing it.

I went home and stayed awake until about three o'clock the next morning looking over what Don had given me and remembering what he'd said. I definitely felt challenged. But I also felt angry and more than a little put down. I'd tried to impress him with the fact that I was, after all, a professional writer with three published books to my credit. Granted, they were children's stories for an educational publisher but Don had not even acknowledged that much.

As morning approached, I had a minor breakthrough. I realized that all my life I had resented people putting things out as gospel truth when it was only their opinion. I still recall a history teacher I had in high school who epitomized this kind of behavior for me. Once I made the mistake of questioning him on a remark he'd made about the Pullman Strike; he'd said that the strikers deserved getting shot and beaten because they had acted illegally. When I foolishly asked him to explain this — I was a champion of the proletariat even then! — he snapped back, "It's true because I say it is, and if you want to get a passing grade in this class you'd better get that through your head."

The sample writing Don had given me to study was at the opposite pole from that. Even while presenting useful, relatively objective information, the sample possessed a tone of humility that I found refreshing and supportive. It did, in fact, seem to acknowldge me, and in this acknowledgment it enlisted my interest. For example, there were three pages from a book about building your own house. The writer had an entire chapter on what a first-time builder might be feeling, his or her fears, how when you are first learning to drive nails with a hammer you can't give up just because you bend a few or whack your thumbs a time or two. The writing convinced me of two things: first, that the author had been a beginner once himself, and second, that he cared enough about me to share the difficulties he'd faced and overcome. Ultimately, the book was as much about human nature as it was about building a house. The author took me by the hand and led me through the self-doubt,

You may write for the joy of it, but the act of writing is not complete in itself. It has its end in its audience.

— Flannery O'Connor

bruises, and blisters that I'd inevitably have to face if I was to take on this adventure. He also told me how to select lumber, frame a wall, put up drywall, and everything else that goes into building. But the human part really impressed me.

The writing touched me in a way I hadn't expected. I felt that this writer cared about me — or at least cared about people. He had taken the time to think about what it means to take in new information like this and attempt to apply it. He was the kind of teacher I longed to have when I was growing up, somebody who could feel my frustration at trying new things and not being quite able to do them the first time around. He was the kind of person who appreciated what we all go through to move from ignorance to knowledge about a particular skill or subject. What showed through was his love for people, and in doing that he won my love.

As a reader, I wanted to know the author better. He literally lit up my life when he shared his own experiences with me. I loved finding out what he went through when he framed up his first wall only to discover he'd misread the blueprint and had cut fifteen studs the wrong length, the result being that he had to start all over again. The story told me that he was a human being just like me, and if he could build a house — false starts, errors, and all — then I was pretty certain I could do the same.

So this was what Don meant about acknowledging the reader!

The next morning I called in sick at work and locked myself in my study. I began rewriting my book about home schooling. And what I very quickly discovered was that the way of writing Don described was a perfect model for the kind of teaching I wanted to encourage in my book. I'd written my first draft in what I call a "Campbell's Soup can" style — simple, straightforward, but without a personal voice. With this new way of writing, I now had a perfect marriage between form and function. I not only told my readers what to do to take their kids out of public school and educate them at home themselves, I told them about my own experiences doing that. I told them what was scary about it and what they could do to handle that part of it.

I wrote about thirty pages over the next day and a half, cutting work for the rest of the week, and mailed them off to Don. A few days later he telephoned to say how much he liked what I'd done. When I went back for our second meeting, we met at his home in North Berkeley. I was surprised to discover where he lived. It was a big, two-story place on a quiet street, with a small backyard and about six bedrooms. He lived there with his wife, Eugenia, three children, and — I learned later — almost always at least one houseguest.

Eugenia sat in on our meeting. Don said he wanted her to sit in because she was the mother of the three kids who lived with them and he thought we should know the perspective of a person who was a little nervous about going against convention. Eugenia had a long list of questions and concerns, which she offered generously, allowing us to flesh out the book so that even a person with great concerns about doing the right thing by their kids would have their questions addressed.

When I went home that night, I did so with a good book outline and a contract in my possession. When I sat down to write the next day, I also discovered something else: I now had an imaginary reader. Whenever I settled into writing, an image of Eugenia came to mind, sitting there in the same room with me as big as life. Like a heroine in a favorite movie, she came alive for me, questioning, prodding, expressing her worries, then waiting for my replies. This was a brand-new experience for me, and the more I worked with it, the more I liked it. My writing became more lively and colorful. It also became much clearer, while providing a teaching model for the readers of the book. The style I was evolving, out of the sheer desire to answer Eugenia's questions, was exactly the kind of teacher-student relationship I thought had to be developed if we were going to improve education in our country.

The more I wrote, the more I realized that by writing this way I no longer felt quite so lonely. One of the things that causes most writers a lot of problems is that it is such a lonely profession. If you're to write, it means there's nobody looking over your shoulder to tell you

No matter how true I believe what I am writing to be, if the reader cannot also participate in that truth, then I have failed.

— Madeleine L'Engle

what to do or when to do it. You have to do all that for yourself. I suppose in the same way that you can create an imaginary reader, most writers also create an imaginary boss who keeps them on track with deadlines. (People often ask me how I discipline myself to write as many books as I have done over the years. I tell them that it isn't discipline at all; it's simple fear. I call it "keeping the wolf from the door.")

The book, titled *No More Public Schools,* was published six months later and sold more than thirty thousand copies over the next three years. It wasn't a best-seller but its relative success encouraged me to quit my job and commit myself to writing full-time. Over the next five years, I published three more books with Don and became his principal editor. I worked on several other authors' books with him, rewriting them when authors couldn't, or wouldn't, do the same.

One of the things I learned during those years was that very few people knew how to write in this personal style that Don was honing in his publishing business. Some even resisted it. When we had editorial meetings with new writers, the subject always got around to past writing experience. I remember one man we worked with, a health practitioner in his early fifties, who said that most of the writing he'd previously done was for school.

"You know," he explained, "in school they tell you to keep yourself out of the writing. Be objective. Back up anything you say with plenty of quotes from recognized experts in the field."

It was clear that a great big piece of writing has been left out for most of us. Good writing for school almost always meant that you were supposed to keep your own voice out of it. Mostly, teachers were interested in discovering whether or not you were paying attention, and how much or how little you had assimilated about what they'd tried to teach you. Personal opinions and firsthand experiences were a no-no, and if anyone ever taught us about acknowledging the reader, I for one completely missed it.

Oddly enough, we've known about this principle of considering the reader as a whole person for centuries. Reading the ancient Greeks, we discover that Sophocles talked a lot about it in the *Poetics,* though he was applying these principles mostly to theater. He talked about "entertaining" the audience, not only emotionally but intellectually, and that it was our ability to reach the person in the audience and to use their ability to laugh and cry, love and fear, that made the difference between good writing and bad. Sophocles didn't know about writing nonfiction but the same principles apply there, too. The good novelist knows it too, that if he or she doesn't touch the reader's heart the book just isn't going to work.

I've worked with budding novelists and short-story writers, however, whose stories suddenly took on a new life, thanks to this very simple insight about developing imaginary readers. When they finally did establish an imaginary reader, the other characters in their stories came alive, too. "It's sometimes like working with a whole roomful of people," one writer told me. "Some of them get to be characters in my books, but there's at least one (the imaginary reader) whom only I know about."

Even as I write these words, what comes to mind is that scene in the public library so many years ago, when I stood up in front of a group of young people and, with knees shaking, read from my book. It was the first time I experienced the role of the reader, and the responsibility we have as authors to consider how they are affected, or not affected, by what we say and how we say it.

One of my author friends once told me, "You have to fall in love with your readers. You have to realize that without their intellectual capacities, as well as their capacities to feel all the feelings you feel, you've got nothing to work with."

Core Concept

In school we learn grammar and structure and getting the facts right. But what gets left out of these early lessons in writing is the most essential of all — that language is a partnership between writer and reader. Learn that lesson and your writing will become electric.

Writing is always a partnership between author and reader, then, and if you somehow miss that, your work is probably not going to be successful. This is not to say that you give readers what they want or expect. When you do that, you're no longer a writer, you're a "hack." It always makes me more than a little angry when I hear television producers arguing that they "only give viewers what they want." In the first place, it's simply not true. They give viewers what they can most easily get their attention with — sex and violence. Such scenes hypnotize us all. And if we are mostly offered only such imagery, we quickly become addicted. For television producers to argue that they're giving us what we want is about the same as the drug pusher who argues that he's giving his customers what they want. Neither group cares about the long-term welfare of their customers or the kind of community values their efforts are encouraging.

When we let ourselves love our readers, they know it. I know it when I read something by an author who acknowledges and respects me. A couple of summers ago, while teaching a workshop in southern Oregon, I asked people in the class to write a twenty-minute description of their imaginary readers. One man, Gil, finished in about ten minutes, then sat back and waited for the others to get through. When we were getting ready to read our efforts aloud, I was pretty certain this guy hadn't done much. How wrong I was! When I asked for volunteers to read, his hand was the first one to shoot up.

He sat back and in a slow, quiet voice read his description of his imaginary reader. He told briefly of growing up on a farm in Texas. His family was Mexican-American and they worked the big farms all over the United States. But mostly they were based on this large farm in Texas.

He told about his "Tío Juan," with whom he had a very special relationship. He described one day out in the field on the tractor with him. It was a big tractor, one of the giant John Deeres they used for plowing and pulling harrows to prepare the soil for planting. Gil was a little boy then, about seven or eight, and he was leaning against the fender as his uncle drove the tractor. Gil wrote:

> My Tío Juan is my good listener. He takes his time and moves his soft brown eyes in my direction, tilting his head over to listen to me. We are on his tractor plowing a cornfield, and he stops the old John Deere to hear what I'm saying. He gives me his full grown-up attention. Taking off his straw hat he wipes his wide sweaty brow with the back of his hand. His eyes wrinkle up as he gives me a generous smile. This big gentle man makes me feel completely safe, so I proceed to tell him just anything. He runs his fingers through his thinning hair. The hot Texas sun makes him squint, so he puts his well-worn hat back on. My sharing makes him laugh — like a kid himself — and then he says, "No viejo, no tengas cuidado — yo te lo doy."

As he finished reading the piece to us, Gil explained, "He always called me old man — viejo — a kind of tender term of endearment and respect. I don't know why. He always said I knew more than any child should know."

When Gil wrote, he wrote to his memory of Tío Juan. He wrote in gratitude for the love and respect this gentle, caring man gave the little child so many years before. A tenderness and warmth in his writing touched the reader's soul so delicately and subtly, like a knowing look between lovers across the room — or maybe like a man stopping a big tractor in the middle of a hot Texas cornfield to hear what a child had to say.

As a reader I want to be entertained, edified, and informed. But I also want to feel that I know the author. Judging by the books that enjoy the biggest readerships, I'm not alone in this. In the 1960s through the late 1970s, we changed a lot in our reading habits. Along with challenging people in power, like politicians, lawyers, manufacturers, doctors, and even educators, we started looking for a different way to measure trust. We no longer believed that if a person had risen to a position of great power they were trustworthy. But if we couldn't determine trustworthiness according to their status in life or the little letters after their names or the school they went to, what could we use to determine it? I know that the answer for me was how they came across to me as a person. Why were they in medicine or politics? What did they get out of being a top lawyer besides power and financial gain? If they could touch me on a human level, I was much more willing, first, to be drawn to them personally, and second, to begin listening very carefully to what they had to say. The one thing I could trust was personal truth — and this had something to do with how they felt about their work, how well integrated it was with the rest of their life.

I'm not saying that everything is a matter of personal opinion, or that only personal truth is important. As a person, I might like a woman or man who does brain surgery, but if I'm going to have them saw a chunk out of my skull and fiddle around with my gray matter, I also want to make certain they know their craft. Trust is personal, there's no doubt about it. And the person I trust is not necessarily going to be the one you trust. The bottom line, I suppose, is that particularly in writing there is no ultimate authority. Being such a personal thing, trust isn't even remotely possible until the author puts himself or herself on the line and lets you know who they are.

With that in mind, writers need to know how to talk to their readers. The imaginary reader is one of the best ways I know to do that because having such a reader in mind as you write is a constant reminder that you are not doing all this work in a vacuum. At some point, if you do it well, your writing is going to be out there for thousands of people to read, and so, in a very real way, we connect with these readers across time and space. The imaginary reader is a conduit to them, and as such, it is as critical a part of the whole writing process as a telephone line or microwave broadcasting system is to communicating with friends across the country.

WRITING EXPLORATION #4
CREATE YOUR IMAGINARY READER

When you set out to develop an imaginary reader, do so with as much care as you'd take to develop a character for a novel or to research the life of a major personality in a biography. Many people start with a person from their past or one in their life now, like Gil, whose imaginary reader was his Uncle Juan. But even if it is somebody you're familiar with, take the time to use your writing skills to get them down on paper. To do this, make use of everything you've done up to now. Put yourself into your place of solitude, focus on your list of the senses so that you can describe what your imaginary reader looks like: What's the color of their hair, eyes, skin? How old is this person? Where do they live? What does their living space look like? What's their relationship to you? How do you feel in their presence? What do they feel about you? What's their personal history?

Just because you're doing this writing for yourself and will probably never share it with anyone else, don't get sloppy. You're the reader and the writer in this case, so make certain you're respecting both. My own experience with creating an imaginary reader is that the more real I can make him or her, the more they literally take root in my unconscious. Even though you may never share with your readers the fact that you have an imaginary reader, there will be a big difference between the writing you do with one and the writing you do without one.

I'm not sure that Ernest Hemingway had an imaginary reader, though I strongly suspect he did. Often his writing sounds like a postcard home, written to a friend he's known a long time. I've always believed his imaginary reader was the sister he talked about in his early Michigan stories, with whom he had a rather tender and protective relationship. He might or might not have been aware that he was doing it, but there's such a strong sense of engagement between author and reader that I'm certain he was doing it on some level.

Whatever the case, Hemingway knew the power of the author knowing things that were important to the story but that might or might not directly appear in it. In an interview in the legendary *Paris Review* in 1958, he said, "I always try to write on the principle of the iceberg. There is seven-eighths of it under water for every part that shows." The imaginary reader is in that seven-eighths of the iceberg that doesn't show.

It's best to write about your imaginary reader until he or she or they begin to take on a life of their own, the way a well-drawn character in a good novel does. Once you've breathed life into them, you've got a writing ally who'll be at your beck and call whenever you need them. When you sit down to write, take whatever time you need to get that reader in focus. Then pretend you're talking to them. Ask them for feedback: about the book idea, the plot, the way you composed the last paragraph or the last sentence. And then learn to listen for feedback. It will come if you give it time. So give it time.

Having an imaginary reader is, by the way, different from what editors and writers mean when they talk about identifying your readership. Both are important but the imaginary reader is usually much more personal, an ally whom you can consult even about such matters as who your readership is. Identifying your readership can vary from book to book, depending on the kind of writer you are, but it's generally a much more logical process than creating an imaginary reader.

When you identify your readership, you're simply asking, who is this book for? What segment of the population might be interested in it? For example, the readership for this book is anybody who wants to become a writer, or any writer who wants to hone his or her skills. If I was writing a book about personal health, my readership would be anybody concerned about maintaining their health. The readership for a book about raising children with high self-esteem would obviously be parents with young kids, or possibly parents who are contemplating having kids, or grandparents, educators, and social workers.

I cannot begin to tell you how many books I've seen get into trouble and not find their niche in the marketplace because their authors weren't clear about this. One in particular stands out in my mind as an example. It was a book about how our educational system fails to teach anything about financial well-being. Certainly this was an excellent issue. But throughout the book, the author switched whom he was talking to. Sometimes it was obvious he was addressing educators. At other times he addressed parents with young children. At other times he talked to people who wanted to know how to get rich. Reading it was like trying to look at a beautiful landscape through a telescope with a cloudy lens. By failing to sharpen his focus on one reader, the author didn't get any of them. The book could have sold more than one hundred thousand copies to any one of those readership groups; as it was, it ended up selling less than a tenth of that total before it was taken out of print.

Sometimes, your imaginary reader and your focused readership are one and the same, and that will make your job a lot easier. I actually have a group of imaginary readers I consult. The one I use in this book is a composite of several people: my younger brother, who is already an excellent writer and occasionally publishes articles in fine woodworking magazines; a woman in her late forties who attended a workshop I taught and is working on what's going to be an excellent historical novel; and a cousin of mine in Ohio who loves writing but really has a struggle disciplining herself to do it. And, of course, I always include the editor who bought my first nonfiction book, Don Gerrard. In addition, there are a couple of imaginary readers whom I don't share with the world; they demand anonymity.

Occasionally, people have trouble with another kind of imaginary reader — and that's the "inner critic." I doubt that there is a single writer who doesn't have an inner critic, but some of us have ones that are a lot tougher than others. In a few cases I've found that the inner critic is responsible for keeping some very talented writers from even beginning their projects. And there are others whose inner critics kept their writing styles so rigid and dull that nobody could stand to read them; they opened up and developed their writing only when they could finally make peace with their tyrannical inner critics. But that's the subject of the next chapter.

CHAPTER FIVE

Making Peace with Your Inner Critic

It takes courage to do what you want. Other people have a lot of plans for you. Nobody wants you to do what you want to do.

— Joseph Campbell

"Every time I sit down to write," Mark said, "there's this part of me that says, 'Who do you think you are! You're not a writer.' And then I get real defiant, like I'm going to show him! I'm going to push on through it. Then I get into this compulsive thing, what I call my grunt mode, where I start going back over my writing with a fine-toothed comb, making certain I've crossed every t and dotted every i. I keep going over every sentence to make certain there are no errors. It becomes almost a life and death issue with me, as if I have to make it perfect. I'm a great grammarian. I've got a dozen reference books telling me exactly how to construct a sentence. My spelling is perfect; it's my big guns against this inner voice that tells me I'm not a writer."

"I know that one," somebody else said. "But I have to confess I'm no grammarian."

"You're lucky," Mark continued. "Because I never get past the first page. I tear every sentence apart, naming every part of speech, even diagramming it sometimes. That's where the whole thing ends — with me obsessively poring over the mechanics of every sentence, every paragraph. But no matter how many times I go over it, I always find something new to correct. Then I realize I'm banging my head against a stone wall, analyzing and rewriting and analyzing and rewriting all over again. Sometimes I never get more than a paragraph down, and finally I give up because no matter how hard I work at it, I can always find more mistakes or ways a sentence could be made better."

"Wasn't it D.H. Lawrence," a woman named Barbara said, "who talked about his coal-miner father who made fun of his literary ambitions, saying that he could never make an honest living that way, that it wasn't a manly thing to do? As I understand it, there was a part of Lawrence, even long after he had published many novels, that always felt that way and never quite felt comfortable writing, even though, on the other hand, he loved it. Sometimes I feel like that. I've written poems and short stories and even had a lot of them published. But every time I sit down to write, I can hear my father saying, 'For this your mother and I made all our sacrifices to send you to college!' The only time I feel halfway okay about what I do is when I get paid for an article, so that's why I write articles, I guess, and neglect my poetry."

The people talking were participants in early workshops I taught. It was when I first introduced the inner reader material to these groups. To my astonishment and embarrassment, instead of coming up with supportive inner readers, about half of the participants came up with these severe inner critics, figures like strict and disapproving teachers or parents who still had a grip on them that they couldn't break.

In spite of my efforts to encourage them to put these harsh inner critics aside and create imaginary readers who would be understanding and supportive, there were always a couple of people in any workshop who just couldn't do it. Whenever they relaxed enough to get themselves into the mood to write, their harsh inner critics always butted in, rudely and aggressively, inhibiting all their creative efforts. If they could write at all, their work generally came out wooden and lifeless, boring to read, painfully stilted.

I always went home after these workshops convinced there were people whose inner critics were so fierce and tenacious that they'd never be able to write, their every creative effort squelched. It troubled me. Partly it troubled me because I knew I had an inner critic or two of my own who I suspected were making it tough for me at times.

The more I thought about this, the more upset and worried I felt, because when I sat down to really think about it, I couldn't quite grasp my own inner critics. I knew part of it, had even learned to use them to my advantage in some cases. But when I tried to nail them down the way many people in my workshops did, they eluded me at every turn. And then one night, around three A.M., I had a vivid dream about my older brother, John, and me. As is my habit, I got up, stumbled into my writing studio, and turned on the word processor. When my dreams are that vivid, I like to write them down right away. The fresher they are, the better.

The dream involved running for political office with my older brother, and I kept getting him mixed up with John F. Kennedy. At one point he'd be Kennedy, and at another time he'd be just my brother John. Like Kennedy, he stood up in front of huge crowds and gave glorious speeches that brought hundreds of people to their feet, applauding. In the dream, I sat on the stage beside the podium, watching the crowd and feeling very proud and awed by my brother's brilliance, privileged to be there on the stage with him.

As he drew near the end of the speech, having listed all his qualifications and the many contributions he'd already made to the community, he said, "Now, I'd like to make a surprise announcement." He turned and gestured for me to join him at the podium, then in a booming voice proclaimed, "I am announcing today that my brother Hal will be my running mate in the coming election."

At this point he turned the podium over to me. I knew I was supposed to stand up and make a speech but I was totally unprepared. This whole thing was a complete surprise to me. I stared out at that sea of faces, eagerly looking up and waiting for me to speak.

I froze. I opened my mouth but no words came. Horrified, I heard only this croaking sound over the public address system, a grotesque sound like something from a wounded animal. Faces in the crowd stared back at me quizzically, then turned to each other. Pandemonium spread through the audience as people got up and filed out of the room, pushing and shouting.

My brother shoved his way up to the podium and shouted for them to stop, to come back, but they didn't. That's where the dream ended, with me standing at the podium beside my brother, feeling completely frustrated, powerless, and humiliated.

> Core Concept
>
> ---
>
> It's ironic to discover that the critics who stop us in our tracks are within us — and that being the case we need to ask ourselves why we do this. If we indeed own our critics, then it means we have a choice — to cling to them or not. We don't need to push them away. On the contrary, we need to let them go.

As I finished recording this dream, I realized that it had a complement in real life. My therapist, many years before, had pointed out to me that I saw myself as insignificant next to my brother

John. I had learned early on that this was the safest role for me to play in the family. My parents idealized him, perhaps because he was born three years after doctors told my mother that they could never have a baby. When John did come, they must have looked upon his birth as a miracle, the fulfillment of a dream they had thought they would have to abandon. He was everything to them, precocious, strong, physically perfect, a darling baby and a godsend. My coming, a year later, was almost anticlimactic, if not bewildering to them. They never knew quite what to make of me. I was a complete surprise. So John easily maintained his already well established role as the star of the family.

One day, when I was perhaps ten years old, I overheard my mother talking to my aunt, who lived half a block down the street from us, back in the suburbs of Detroit where I grew up. I heard mother say, "Hal is our black sheep of the family. He came out of a very different mold than the rest of us." She laughed when she said this but she also said it with such a degree of conviction that I knew she believed it was true.

Years later, my therapist would explain to me that this statement and my bewilderment about it became a self-fulfilling prophecy, which began with my parents' surprise by my birth. From the moment I came into life I was cast in the role of the outsider — of a "different mold" than the rest of my family. Everything John was, I was not. He was looked upon as the great student and intellectual; I was seen as, well, certainly not much of a student and of questionable mental abilities. Where he was the extrovert, I was the brooding introvert, prone to daydreaming instead of taking care of business in the real world. Where he went along with the program, doing his best to fulfill our parents' expectations for him, I rebelled.

I knew how to do one thing very well, and that was to support my brother in every way I could. Early on I discovered an invisible line I must never cross over. That line had to do with staying a step or two behind John, staying in his shadow, applauding him whenever he did anything worthy. It was as if I was doing it less for him than for our parents, however. I sensed that it was absolutely essential to never bring into question the fact that John was number one.

Most of the time I did a pretty good job of fulfilling my assigned role in the family. But behind it all was this terrible fear. I was on a dangerous mission, always one step away from an emotional disaster. If I made the mistake of taking that single step I would topple over into endless depths, lost forever. What made it worse was that there was an inner drive that was always tempting me to take that step, regardless of the consequences.

There were things I yearned to do but could not risk for fear that I would overshadow my brother John. I loved working with my hands, doing artwork and writing. But I dared not commit myself fully to any of these activities because I feared that I might do something better than John. So when I did them at all, I did them in secrecy, often destroying what I did or hiding them away where nobody else would find them. It was a painful secrecy.

In the dream I had that day, this same fear choked off my own voice, even at the point when my older brother invited me to share his glory. I had so thoroughly learned my lesson, that is, what I must do to be valued and protected and loved within the family, that even when the opportunity was handed to me on a golden platter I could not step forward. I couldn't make use of the opportunity because by speaking up I risked challenging my parents' perceptions of John's and my identities.

What the dream told me was that most of us have inner critics, and that they can exert an extremely powerful influence on our creative lives. Furthermore, they can have many faces, and are often just one part of a family emotional dynamic that has many interlocking pieces. In my case, there was a trade-off, what my therapist called a "secondary gain," about standing in my brother's shadow. In fact, I sometimes wonder if it wasn't all secondary gain, because I found very little primary satisfaction in being dumber, less talented, and less good-looking than my brother John. I reined myself in and made myself virtually invisible so that my parents could feel safe in their illusions about him.

When you dream, you dialogue with aspects of yourself that normally are not with you in the daytime and you discover that you know a great deal more than you thought you did.

— Toni Cade Bambara

The things kids ordinarily did to win their parents' love, that is, doing the very best they could with the talents they had, were taboo for me. Holding them back was the way I won their love. The only way I could feel valued in the family was to be less than I could be.

My therapist told me that this did not mean I was doomed forever to hold back. On the contrary, she said, we often find our greatest abilities by looking more closely at these early patterns in our lives and then transforming them. She was a clever counselor. As we worked together over the months, I concluded that I could take advantage of my early teachings by serving others who, like my older brother, were "stars" of the family — in this case, stars of the larger family to which I'd become attached in my adulthood.

In the early 1960s I discovered I was good at working with other writers, and I enjoyed working with them. Most of the authors I worked with were high-profile lecturers or workshop teachers. Publishers wanted books from them because they were highly visible and their visibility helped to sell books. But these same people often didn't have either the time or the ability to write their own books. That's where I came in. I quickly learned that I could work with these people in the same way that I'd worked with my brother in my childhood. I learned to study the communication style of each person and write in their voice. I got so good at it that many of the stars I worked with couldn't distinguish between my writing and theirs. Because they couldn't, I became virtually invisible to them. Ironically, the very talent that made me valuable to them also made it extremely difficult to recognize my contribution. My efforts usually went unrewarded — except financially. I began to make a good living.

I took a great pride in my invisibility. If I had an ego investment in my work, it was in giving people exactly what they wanted. I sometimes saw my role as something like an actor's, playing out other people's scripts, making their work look as good as I could make it look, but always hiding who I really was. Publishers loved me and rewarded me well for my efforts.

Writing alone, writing my own books, was always a painful process. Even today, as I write these words, there's a level of anxiety, a sense that I'm risking much, that there is danger in putting myself on the line this way. But the more conscious I've become of my inner critic(s), and the more clearly I've been able to see them, the easier it has become to work with my own craziness. I see and hear my inner critics in the background. They don't tell me "don't do this" — not exactly. They only look pained and bewildered when I speak from my own heart and a part of me goes forward and does it anyway, in spite of feeling anxious about hurting them.

I often think that creativity is a lot like intuition in that it's something we are born with, something that's always there right under our noses. Learning to tap its many riches isn't so much a matter of learning as unlearning.

I have this inner guide, a Native American figure, a tool maker, I call Awahakeewah. Some years ago, I was in crisis. I had a major dose of that dread disease they call "writers' block." Whenever I sat down to write, I drew a total blank. It was as if I had lost my ability to even think.

On one particularly gloomy day, I did the only constructive thing I could do under the circumstances; I put on my earphones, a quiet environmental tape of ocean waves lapping gently against the shore, and meditated. The sound of lapping waves drowned out the background noise of traffic and ringing phones in my office — which was on a busy street in Palo Alto, California, at the time — and after a half hour or so, Awahakeewah began to come forward in my consciousness.

"What's going on with me?" I asked.

He smiled gently, understandingly. "You must understand," he said, "your creativity does not belong to you. It is part of the Creative Spirit that makes us all, that gives us life and that gives the entire universe its form. You have been given your small share of the Creative Spirit but you are treating it as if you owned it. It is not yours to own. So get the hell out of its way!"

This conversation seemed so real to me, and so unexpected, that I suddenly popped out of the deep meditative state I'd sunk into and asked myself aloud, "How am I standing in its way?"

The answer didn't come immediately. But something was knocked loose and that same day, probably within an hour or two of this encounter, I began writing again. The words and ideas came quickly and easily, flowing out on the paper effortlessly. At the time, I was working on a book for another person, but a project of my own, which I'd been struggling with for over a year, made its first stirrings and broke through.

Remembering Awahakeewah's counsel, I remind myself that our creativity is a sacred trust. If we are blocking it, consciously or unconsciously, through the inner critic or any other psychological impediment we're employing, it's almost as if we're committing a kind of sin. My guide's teaching is that we are never more generous, never more blessed, than when we give of ourselves through that little piece of the Creative Spirit that lives in each of us. Letting our inner critics stand in the way is self-indulgent, maybe even narcissistic.

I don't know if I'll ever be completely free of my inner critic, of this dynamic that tells me that my only value is through serving others. In so many ways, it has been one of my greatest teachers. And I think that maybe this is the way it is for all of us. We can't deny our inner critics. We can't pretend they're not there and push them away, hoping to replace them with ideal inner readers. I believe they live on within our private inner worlds, and as we get to know them better we can march them out, make them characters in our personal stories. In doing so, we take one or two steps back and can allow them to grow, to reveal to us the fears and misunderstandings that make them want to act as they do.

Core Concept

The writer treats the inner life, whether painful or blissful, as the raw material of the craft, just as clay is to the potter. While we need to heal our wounds so that they don't cripple us, we also need to realize that without their imagery and tensions we'd have little to draw upon for our creative life. Our inner critics are part of that inner landscape, waiting to be transformed through our craft.

In that inner world where I still hold those parents who were so afraid I'd step out of my brother's shadow, I've given them permission to come alive. I've let them become the rich characters, like the characters in a good novel, who have lives separate from mine. I no longer see them just from the perspective of how they've made my creative life difficult. I see my mother — the inner one — in her childhood, wanting so much to idealize her dad, to hold him high in spite of knowing a dark secret that shattered her image of him whenever she let it through. And I see my inner father as resentful of his own parents, angry with his father for dying too soon. My inner father, like me, served his brother, putting him through medical school to fulfill his mother's dream. Both my father and my uncle clung to their own fears, and in doing so they held back the truth that would have set them free.

I play with their fears in my mind, seeing through them, feeling their grief and their bewilderment, putting it down on paper, in my journals, and sometimes in stories I write. The richer and more real they become in my mind, the more I feel free of them. It has become a strange kind of cocreative process, living with each other in the service of a power greater than all of us put together.

I don't believe we find the path to freedom and to our own greatest gifts by complaining and bemoaning our battles with these demons we call our inner critics; rather, we find freedom by transforming them and making them into our teachers. These inner critics are the known paths of our lives, and as much as we may hate them and feel ourselves limited by them, we cling to them because they are familiar. We jump into the unknown when we dare to make them more real, not less, and it's then that we abandon the familiar path and go out on our own, fully embracing our own creativity. We can do so by letting these characters have their own lives, separate from us, and then choosing to — as Joseph Campbell so often advised — break out and "follow your bliss pattern, quitting the old place, starting your hero journey, following your bliss."

WRITING EXPLORATION #5
EMBRACE YOUR INNER CRITIC(S)

We conquer our inner critics not by shoving them aside or pretending they don't exist but by fully embracing them. When you can see the whites of their eyes, hear their words, and describe their threatening or demeaning looks, they become yours, no longer the invisible puppet masters pulling your strings.

You will gain freedom from these critics and even make them your allies when you can clearly picture them in your mind's eye and even write about them. Every great novelist knows this trick and ultimately uses their inner critics as characters in their stories — making them villains, clowns, subjects for ridicule, or pathetic victims of their own arrogance or shortsightedness. Sometimes they even help them resolve the inner conflicts that make them cruel adversaries, so that they grow up to be admirable people.

If you are a fiction writer, describe your inner critic(s) in as much detail as you can. Or write a story in which their idiosyncratic behavior gets them into trouble, forcing them to expose their shortcomings, and possibly even change.

Nonfiction writers can do something similar by looking at the themes the inner critics represent. First, get as close as you can to your inner critics by doing quick character sketches of them. Then write a description of the theme they bring up for you. Make it your focus for an article or book idea. For example, if you grew up with an abusive parent who criticized you all the time and undermined your self-esteem, briefly outline an article or book to write that would help a person who had experienced something similar to you.

Your inner critics will always be with you. They will not go away — but they can be transformed. Once transformed, they become a source of power for you rather than a source of weakness and fear.

CHAPTER SIX

Coming to
Our Senses

How good is man's life, the mere living!

How fit to employ

All the heart and the soul and the senses forever in joy!

— Robert Browning

The phrase "windows to the soul" sticks in my mind at this moment. My impression is that I've heard those words repeated in a hundred different love poems. Maybe not. At the same time, I don't believe I'm being very original when I think of the five senses as the way into that most elusive inner core of our being.

Does the soul really give a damn about the orange hues of a desert sunset or the crystalline, luminescent moon hovering over a snowcapped mountain peak? Apparently it does. When I think back to the truly special moments in my life, I immediately recall a wondrous concert of the senses — the soft hush, hush, hush of gentle waves lapping against the shore on Lake Michigan when I was a child, the cry of a gull hanging on the wind, white wings tipping against a flawless blue sky. And many years later, I recall lying with my lover, our sleeping bags rolled out next to a lush green meadow high in the Sierras, gazing up into the infinitude of the heavens dotted with brilliant specks of silver, a chorus of coyotes telegraphing their lonely songs across the miles. What lures me back to the deep satisfaction of such moments is the color, the sound, the scents, the sweet subtle touch of a warm breeze on my skin. I've often thought how paradoxical it is that our spirits leap to the delight of the senses. It's ironical to think that the soul, which is not supposed to be tempted by the delights of the flesh, would find such pleasure in the senses. I can't help but wonder if the moralists who would have us deny the body's pleasures haven't deliberately misled us, thus hiding a valuable passage to the soul.

Core Concept

Words and phrases that speak to the senses — sight, sound, taste, smell, and touch — have an almost miraculous ability to narrow the distance between writer and reader. In the process, they can also take us closer to our spiritual essence.

This morning when I sat down to write, I turned to some pages in an old journal, dated several years back. The entry that caught my eye described a powwow I'd attended on the Stanford University campus. Each year Indians come there from every corner of the country to celebrate. That day, I stood at the edge of the football field watching the dancers in the center. Native Americans from a dozen different nations, many of them dressed in traditional costumes, moved in a dusty circle around the track at the edge of the field. It was a blazing hot day, the sun burning down on the dancers, who appeared to bask in its rays. Flashes of brightly dyed fabric, red and turquoise blue and yellow and green, swept by as the dancers flowed slowly past, following the rhythm of drums whose reverberations filled the air, vibrating even the ground under our feet, like the heartbeat of Mother Earth herself. Many dancers wore anklets, each with as many as a dozen small brass bells, that jingled in a magnificently clangorous chorus with each step, the sound mingling with the steady life-giving beat of the drums.

I watched the dancers' feet as they moved in an endless circle around the field and realized they were doing something very different from what I had thought they were. Each step was deliberate and purposeful, yet almost a shuffle, as if to caress Mother Earth and as if to feel her skin, to sense her life, her spirit. It suddenly became clear to me that their movements were not intended as an exhibition, as I'd thought, but as a way of experiencing something I could not see. The dance was about touching the earth, letting her know we are here, feeling her under us as a live being whose support and love we must celebrate.

Here, all the senses — sight, sound, touch, smell, taste — came alive. The colorful costumes, the cacophony of the jingling anklets, the reverberating heartbeat of the drums, the whoops and cries of the dancers, the air rich with the aromas of burning sage, sizzling fry bread, lamb stew bubbling in great pots, and the sweating bodies of the dancers in the summer heat. What I'd give to make a page of type do all that!

Words want to rest on the page much more quietly. These little black squiggles on a white field would prefer just to lie there, abstract and frozen in time. Yet, when I read words associated with the senses, like red, blue, green, jingling, thumping, sour, sweet, velvety, soft, a sensuous breeze over the skin, something is excited very deep inside me. When I recall the jangling clamor of a dozen dancers, each wearing anklets of tiny brass bells, I am transported out of my everyday thoughts. How is it that the mere mention of color or sound, smell, taste, or touch awakens a sense of deeper involvement? What are these inner doors our senses open up to us? With these doors flung open, we invariably step over the threshold, crossing the boundary that previously separated author and reader. We are taken into the other's life, and in the crossing we relinquish our own boundaries.

Back in my college days, I had this friend Jerold who was blind. Something happened during his birth so that he was never able to see anything but a slight sensation of light. He said he could tell if a room was dark or if it was light but that was about all. In spite of his blindness, he wrote poetry with rich dramatic imagery.

One day we were walking across campus between classes. When we walked together he always folded up his white cane, which telescoped down so that it fit in a little leather holster on his belt. He walked close beside me, not quite touching, and no matter how fast I walked he kept up, striding along as if he had perfect sight. He explained to me that he had learned how to jog with a friend who was sighted. They'd worked it out so that his friend sort of "drove" him, taking into account the space Jerold would require to turn a corner, in the same way that you take into account the size of a car when you're behind the wheel. He said it was easy to sense the energy of the other person and move in concert with it, as long as he was no more than three or four feet away. He liked walking fast beside me and not having to be cautious the way he had to be with the tapping cane.

I asked him one time how he could create such coherent imagery in his poetry, since he had never been able to see. He shrugged. "Partly

If you atrophy one sense you also atrophy all the others, a sensuous and physical connection with nature, with art, with food, with other human beings.

— Anaïs Nin

from the feel of things. Partly from other clues — sound, for example. I tell a lot from sound."

"In your poems you always describe colors," I said. "How can you do that if you've never seen color?"

"Seen it?" he asked, obviously somewhat surprised by my question. "Do you think a person depends on his eyes to see color?"

"I would think so," I said.

"Don't you dream in color?" he asked.

"Sure."

"Maybe it's like that. After all, where are your eyes in a dream?"

"I would have a memory of color," I argued, "since I walk around every day with eyes that see. But where would you get the information to know these things?"

"I can't explain it," he admitted. "Maybe the green I see is different than the green you see. I don't know. How would you tell?"

We played a word association game then. I would say a word and he would say the first color that came into his mind: I'd say, "Grass"; he'd reply, "Green." I'd say, "Car"; he'd reply, "Could be any color." I'd say, "Anger"; he'd reply, "Red." I'd say, "Placid, calm"; he'd say, "Blue, sometimes dark blue, sometimes very light blue." I'd say, "Sun"; he'd say, "Yellow, maybe orangish red."

Then we switched it around. I'd name a color, he'd say the first word association that came into his mind. I'd say, "Red"; he'd say, "Excitement, danger, stop." I'd say, "Green"; he'd say, "Landscape, peacefulness, vegetation."

Neither of us ever quite solved the puzzle but something came clear to me from that exchange. It was that a part of us beyond the physical senses responds to suggestions of touch, taste, smell, sight, and sound. My friend Jerold pointed out to me that Helen Keller, who was born without the ability to either hear or see, nevertheless found great pleasure in all the senses through her reading and writing. She once said, "Literature is my Utopia. Here I am not disfranchised. No barrier of the senses shuts me out from the sweet, gracious discourse of my book friends."

My wife and I have two small dogs (Maltese), each weighing about six pounds full grown. Every morning we take them for a long walk on a trail beside an estuary near our home. Although they were originally developed as lap dogs, ours have apparently never read the breeders' manuals because they love nothing better than running free in the great outdoors. We take them to the head of the trail in the car, and when we get near the place where we let them out, they start howling with excitement, crying to get out and run.

Today when I took them out, it was 6:30 in the morning. Cicily, the older of the two dogs, leapt from the car and raced down the short hill to the water's edge just in time to nearly collide with a magnificent blue heron just rising from the edge of the bank. The bird spread its splendid five-foot span of wings and lifted high in the air, the dog craning her neck back and up to watch, eyes wide with amazement, her entire body trembling with awe. When the bird was fully airborne, the dog turned and ran back up the hill to meet me, jumping up on my leg as if to get my attention, to make certain I'd seen what she'd just seen, then running back down the hill at breakneck speed, nose to the ground, racing off in the direction the bird had flown. Maddy, the puppy, followed after her, her short feet barely skimming the ground as she practically took flight herself.

I followed the dogs, who quickly gave up trying to catch the bird, who'd now settled down on the water several hundred yards ahead of us. The two tiny dogs ran back and forth across the trail, noses to the ground, stopping every few minutes to investigate a scent more thoroughly, frequently marking that spot with their own urine. Their delight with this world of scent was expressed in their frolicking movements, turning only occasionally to check with me and make certain I was following. Their ears pricked up, alert, their bushy white tails waving wildly back and forth, held high; they were rapturous, jubilant, their souls singing.

As I followed them, my own spirits soared. Watching them cavort, exploring this world of scent, I could not help but wonder what it was they were finding so delightful. These smells that delighted them were nonexistent for me, and when I let my imagination entertain the possibilities, I must confess that I was grateful for that. I have an idea I might not be able to share their fascination with these perfumes. Even so, the scents obviously speak to something that lifts these small animals' souls and in the process lifts mine.

Whatever it is that delights us about the senses, be it these mysterious smells that elude me even as they enchant my dogs, or the sounds of music that raise my spirits but leave my animals cold, the whole thing is a great mystery to me. By all rights, it does not seem feasible that the evocation of the senses would open these doors to the soul. Even more a contradiction is the notion that words could set the whole thing in motion, and even at times fill the darkness with light and color or the silence with voices and song.

Assuming it's true that our real identity is spiritual, and that we've taken a physical form to learn certain lessons, I'd like to suggest that the puzzles we're here to ponder might ultimately be revealed through the senses. And maybe we've been given language to push the riddle to an even higher level of implausibility, where we are willing to say, after all, that the universe is truly beyond our finite capacities. If we play with language and the senses long enough, we are led to the soul where we can finally say, "I don't know," and be completely at peace with that.

WRITING EXPLORATION #6
SENSORY INTELLIGENCE

Go back and read the first three pages of this chapter, particularly noting the description of the powwow. Carefully note the adjectives describing colors, sounds, tastes, scents, movements, and touch. Notice how these words bring a liveliness to the scenes they describe.

For twenty minutes, describe the room in which you are sitting or any other scene you would like, using as many adjectives as you can that refer to the five senses: sight, sound, scent, taste, and touch. Remember that touch refers both to tactile sensations and to movements of the body.

Whether you are writing fiction, poetry, or nonfiction, your mastery of sense description is one of the most powerful assets you have for engaging your readers. It is one of the core secrets of good creative nonfiction, because it allows you to immerse the reader in a person or situation you are writing about. It is the heart and soul of fiction writing because it is with your mastery of sensory information that characters and scenes come alive.

CHAPTER SEVEN

Our Search for the Elusive Present

To observe without distortion is only possible if there is complete attention with your body, your nerves, your mind, your heart, your ears. Then you will see, if you so attend, that there is no entity or being called the observer. Then there is only attention.

— J. Krishnamurti

Occasionally I'll find a quiet corner at a coffee shop or some other public place where I can write. There is one such place near my home, a café at a small lake. The lake is man-made, near the center of what locals call Shoreline Park. It's a grassy park in the middle of a wetlands preserve of several thousand acres on the edge of San Francisco Bay. You can't swim in the lake but it is a good place to sail small boats because from one o'clock until dusk, there's a strong steady wind that comes in over the bay. In the summer months, with school out, the lake attracts throngs of windsurfers and young sailors who like the relative security and shelter that it provides.

I've always been envious of those people who can take a pad of paper and a pen and write for hours in public places. Like the sailors on this little lake, I seem to need boundaries, a container. As I sat outdoors on this particular day, it was pleasant enough to feel the heat of the sun on my face and the wind in my hair, but I felt frustrated because I couldn't get into the writing I'd planned to do there. With my pen poised above the paper, I had the sense that my thoughts were soaring out beyond my reach and I couldn't lure them in with my pen. If I only had four walls around me and a roof over my head, they couldn't escape.

Core Concept

The closer we can get to the present in our writing, creating a sense of immediacy with our words, the more deeply engaged the reader will be. This holds true whether we are writing a poem, a novel, or even a work of nonfiction in which the author's point of view matters to the reader.

Across the patio, on my left, there was a young couple leaning toward each other over the table. He was sitting with his back to me, wearing a blue blazer and neatly pressed white trousers, which seemed out of place in the summer heat. She wore a two-piece swimsuit. I could only see her bare right shoulder and part of her right leg, the rest blocked by her companion and by a white plastic chair in my line of sight. I could see that their hands were resting on the tabletop close enough to touch, but they were not touching. It was impossible to determine their mood from where I sat but my impression was that there was a great chasm between them that yearned to be bridged.

I watched them for several minutes, looking for clues about what might be going on. Then I heard a shout of alarm, "No!" I turned to my right in time to see a barefoot toddler, dressed only in diapers, running toward the lake, with a young blonde woman in jeans and a red sweatshirt in hot pursuit. There was a five-foot strip of gravel just before the water's edge and as the child hit it she lost her balance, tried to recover, then hurtled forward. A second later she had tumbled face first into the water. The young blonde woman scooped her up, lifted her high and spun her around, laughing, then came galloping back up to the patio where an older woman was standing stiffly, shaking her head and scolding.

The young blonde woman was taking the whole incident of the runaway child very calmly, even making light of it. She held the little girl in her arms and sat down at one of the round plastic tables. The older woman sat down opposite her and even from fifty feet away I could hear them arguing. The younger woman was getting a thorough scolding and the child, who hadn't been upset until then, began to cry, clinging to the blonde woman's bosom and hiding her face from the older woman.

When I turned back to the young couple at the table to my left, I discovered they were gone. Although I looked all around, I could see no sign of them. I was curious about how they could have disappeared so fast. But in an instant I had all but forgotten about them.

There was a single, small sailboat out in the middle of the lake, moving away from me. Its gray hull was heeled way over, at a forty-five degree angle, and the single sailor was leaning way out on the starboard side, counterbalancing against the wind. He drove the boat hard, waves lapping over the gunwales, threatening to swamp the hull. But he went on, coming about only when he had run out of lake, about a half mile away.

I caught myself thinking that there is a peculiar kind of privacy I experience in public places. Being among strangers, I retreat into myself. If I pay close attention, it is easy to see how much I project to the world. I try to quiet my mind, to be more attentive to what's going on around me and for short periods of time I lose myself completely in the scene. As in the Krishnamurti passage at the beginning of this chapter, there ceases to be an observer. I feel myself merge with the landscape, with the activity going on around me.

The trouble is, I can't write in this frame of mind. To write, one has to become a writer, that is, an observer, and this means stepping back, moving just outside the scene. The best I can do is be an observer, observing myself sitting in this molded, white plastic chair, at this round, molded plastic table, watching the sailboat on the lake now heading back in my direction. I am the observer who watches me sitting there, linked to others around me by little more than proximity — the sailor in his boat on the lake, the two women and the child, the man in the blue blazer and the woman in the swimsuit who are no longer there. It's odd how this observer part allows us to merge with the landscape, even lose ourselves in it, yet be there to notice, to take notes.

I have an idea that writers, more than most, know this observer self. I'm not sure how it is for other writers but at times, it is as if my everyday self, the self that takes part in the always-unfolding drama of life, is simply in the service of this other part. Or is it vice versa? The everyday self is the part that wonders about the man in the blue blazer whose hands don't reach out to touch the hands of the woman opposite him. It's the part that reacts to alarm as the toddler loses her balance and plunges head first in the lake. It's the part that feels what it must be like to be a

If you let yourself be absorbed completely, if you surrender completely to the moments as they pass, you live more richly in those moments.

— Anne Morrow Lindbergh

sailor hanging far out over the gunwales of the sailboat heeling sharply in the wind. Without this part that stands outside the scene, could we write at all?

Writing in public places reminds me of the partnership between these two parts of myself — observer and experiencer, if you will. The experiencer part has the strong awareness of possessing a physical body, which separates me from the rest of the world. It's the part that owns the senses through which I become aware of sounds and shapes and smells and scents and texture and movements around me. It's the part that owns the personal history that causes me to fear, celebrate, wonder, or feel conflict about events around me. The observer self is, as far as I can tell, passionless.

Most writers I've known have had a difficult time balancing these two. I remember, long ago, reading an essay by Henri Bergson, the French philosopher and literary critic, who talked about the powers of this observer self. He was talking about the fine line between tragedy or pathos and comedy, and that all we needed to do to transform pathos or tragedy into comedy was to step back into the observer viewpoint. In doing so, we no longer had an emotional investment in the scene. We could smile and let it go because as long as we remained in the observer frame of mind, nobody got hurt. Life would be seen only as an illusion, where the passions that seem so earthshaking to us from our everyday perspective become absurdities.

Immersed in the landscape, lost in the passions of our lives, any sense of separation or of being able to step outside ourselves fades away. Writing alone in a public place, where the passions of life are happening to other people, as they might happen on a stage, I become a voyeur who never gets too deeply involved. My observer self dominates at such moments. And if I respond with alarm or curiosity or any of the other reactions to our lives, it intrudes with its timeless detachment, its jaded, philosophical indifference, reminding me that all is vanity.

When we want to immerse ourselves in a scene and bring the present alive in our reader's mind, the observer self is invaluable. It stands outside us, like a lifeguard ready to dive in and drag us out if it looks like we're going down. And it may be this same part of us that guards over the craft of writing itself, reminding us that only the artful rendering of the raw material of life elevates writing above gossip or telling jokes over a few beers. It's the craft that makes the ordinary universal.

In spite of its disdain for the senses and for what it considers our human shortcomings, the observer self is always reminding me of the quest for the present. Like Krishnamurti, I am reminded constantly that our greatest power lies in our ability to observe without distortion. And we achieve this by giving complete attention to our bodies, our nerves, our minds, our hearts, and our senses. Ironically, that's when the observer vanishes.

It is the greatest of all life's contradictions, perhaps, that when we are most focused on our physical being, we are best able to see beyond it into the nonphysical, the timeless, the universal. What's more, it is from this same "presence of mind/body" that our words best communicate to others. Just as deep meditation takes us to the place where the observer mind dissolves, so the boundaries between reader and writer are dissolved when the latter can help the former focus on the present, on the senses, and on what we are holding in our hearts and minds at the moment.

Core Concept

If our goal is to dissolve the distance between ourselves and our readers, or between our readers and what we want to tell them, then understanding our own perceptions of the present is a required skill. Authors whose works endure know and use this insight often and well.

Language isn't the best way to accomplish this, however. Especially in English, we're constantly forced to use the past tense: "I *was* walking down the street smelling the flowers." It begins to sound contrived if we try to say it in the present: "I *am* walking down the street smelling the flowers." The illusion doesn't work. As I read this sentence, I know the writer isn't doing what he or she is saying. God only knows what he or she is doing at this point! So I'm not taken in. The conclusion is that under the best of circumstances, we writers must create our illusions in the past tense.

Years ago, a novelist I was studying with, Wright Morris, described a trick he'd learned for breaking through writer's block. The trick was to sit down and start writing about exactly what was happening in the present. He said to get as sharply focused and attentive to the present as possible. It might go something like this:

> I am sitting in front of my computer screen, my fingers moving over the keyboard. As they move they make funny little clicking sounds, dull rattles that I find comforting. With each finger motion, a new letter appears on the screen. Letters become words and words become whole paragraphs. The telephone rings off to my left and I resist the pull to answer it. I stop typing as it rings and rings, ten times in all before it stops. I put my hands back on the keyboard but then I start to worry. Who could be calling? What was so urgent to ring ten times?

Though it is the most mundane activity I'm describing, it brings me into the present. I immediately calm down. All the words and images and ideas that normally bounce around in my mind slow down. I become increasingly attentive to my senses, my body, my mind. Oddly enough, when I've accomplished what I set out to do, the reader is transported into my world. Together we enter the illusion of moving more and more into the center. Just as in meditation, we stop watching ourselves living our lives and become life.

All the great sages seem to profess the same thing, from Muhammad and Moses to contemporary thinkers like J. Krishnamurti,

*Just as my
fingers on
these keys
Make music, so
the self-same
sounds
On my spirit
make a music,
too.*

— Wallace Stevens

Abraham Maslow, and Joseph Campbell: "To thine own self be true." Follow your bliss! The way to that self, that bliss, is always through attentiveness to the present. Why it happens is still a mystery to me. But each time it happens to me, each time I accidentally or deliberately bring my attention fully into the present, whether on the page or in real life, I am once again sold on the idea. And if too long a time elapses between actual experiences of such moments, I recite to myself some lines by one of my favorite poets, Wallace Stevens.

WRITING EXPLORATION #7
WRITING INTO THE ELUSIVE PRESENT

At the beginning of this book, I described an exercise I call the Writer's Daily Meditation, or Writing in the Present. If you have been religiously doing this exercise every day, you may have already discovered how it focuses you on the present, revealing your own sensibilities, memories of your past experiences, and how the writing you do during these short sessions can unveil powerful themes and imagery that inspire longer works.

If you haven't been doing this exercise, I strongly urge you to start and to make it a daily habit. In no time, you will discover what many others already have, that this exercise alone can help you reach into your heart and soul to tap your richest creative resources. No other exercise I know can accomplish so much, particularly when you get into the routine of doing it daily — even if that only means fifteen or twenty minutes each morning.

Here are just a few of its many lessons:

1. If you are suffering from writer's block, the exercise will help you overcome this very quickly. When your assignment is to write in the present, no matter what you find there, it becomes impossible not to write. You might

write about how you can't think of a single thing to write
— if that's in fact what you feel. And you'll be surprised
at how good the writing will be.

2. As a writer's meditation, writing in the present will immediately reveal your current frame of mind. If you're
blocked, you may discover not only what's blocking you
but how to move beyond it. Use it regularly as a way of
exploring what it means to you to bring your focus into
the here-and-now. Note that when you write down what
you are experiencing in the present, you are literally
recording where you stand in relationship to the present.
If you keep these writings in a journal — which I highly
recommend — you will be able to refer to it in the future.
Knowing where your mind goes when you relax deeply is
important. If you write fiction, it gives you insights into
personal motivations — both yours and other people's. If
you write nonfiction, it can provide insights into your
thought processes and the importance of recognizing the
processes readers go through.

3. Daily practice of this exercise can also teach you how to
render scenes in the present. For example, one day you
may wish to see what happens when you focus on writing only about the things you see, hear, smell, taste, and
touch in the present. These will be primarily sensual:

the telephone ringing, the sweet scent of flowers in the vase on your desk, the bitter taste of your morning coffee, and how the keys press against your fingertips as you type. At another time, you may focus on writing only about the busyness of your mind: worrying about being late to work if you write for too long, thinking about what you should have said in yesterday's argument with a friend, or daydreaming about an upcoming vacation you're planning. Pay attention to how you feel while you are writing — that is, how *in the present* you are with these different writings. Does writing about your senses immerse you in the present more than memories and daydreams? Read these writings to a friend and see which examples they like best, which bring them closer to your heart and mind, and which take them further away. You may be surprised by the outcome.

4. Use writing in the present as a warmup exercise to get you started when you find all the tasks that you should be doing around the house distract you.

5. Look upon this exercise as your writer's laboratory, revealing to you how what's going on in the present affects what goes down on the page — or doesn't get down on the page, as the case may be. Always keep in

mind that you need not be in a seminar or writing the next Great American Novel to expand your knowledge of the inner craft. That's what this exercise is about.

The instructions are sheer simplicity: Write for ten minutes, describing exactly what is happening in the present for you. If you are stuck, start with the phrase, "I am now putting my pen to the paper..." or "I have now turned on my computer and have begun clacking away at the keyboard, making the little squiggles we call letters come up on the screen...."

CHAPTER EIGHT

Higher Creativity and the Peak Experience

*All other memories of travels, people and my surroundings have paled beside
these interior happenings.... But my encounters with the "other" reality, my
bouts with the unconscious, are indelibly engraved upon my memory.
In that realm there has always been wealth in abundance,
and everything else has lost importance by comparison.*

— C. G. Jung

L ast night I awoke from a dream and for a long time lay in bed
luxuriating under the warmth of the soft down comforter, trying to remember it all. In the dream it was a crisp, fall evening. I
was standing on a dock made of weathered planks as thick as rail-
road ties. It stretched out a hundred feet into a deep, blue lake, a
half mile across and two miles in length. I looked out over the
water to the opposite shore and a dense green wall of cedars. With
the sun dropping below the hills behind me, shadows quickly
spread through the trees and there was a mystical quality about
the landscape, as if it had been drawn not from nature but from
an artist's rendition of a lake. The colors were too intense for a

real landscape, and the entire scene appeared as if frozen in time.

I was there alone, and I had the clear sense that I was no more than ten or twelve years old. I walked out onto the dock and knelt down to untie a rope wrapped around a chock fastened to one of the planks. I dropped the rope down into the bottom of a wooden rowboat bobbing alongside the dock a few feet below me. Then I slipped down over the side into the boat. As it took up my weight, the boat tipped slightly. I adjusted my weight, took a step toward the center seat, and sat down. I shoved away from the dock, swinging the bow out toward the middle of the lake, then took up the oars, lifted them, dipped them into the water, pulled, and the boat slipped forward away from the shore.

I rowed toward the center of the lake, dipping the oars, pulling, lifting them, leaning forward, dipping and pulling, over and over again. The boat moved effortlessly over the water. I rowed until I could no longer see the dock. With each pull of the oars, the boat rose, then fell, on gentle waves. The rhythm of my rowing joined with the rhythm of the waves, rocking my body sensuously, sublimely. I could no longer see the shore nor the sky. I only saw the water all around me, and the worn gray gunwales of the boat on either side of me. I saw the bottom of the boat, narrow planks, damp from the water that had dripped from the oars as I rowed.

As I moved across the lake, something very odd began to happen. I was no longer just the boy in the rowboat. I was also the boat and the lake and the sky. I felt in myself the density and weight of water, teeming with life, every living being, every fish, crustacean, weed, and lily pad a part of me. The boy in the boat, rowing over my surface, was a part of me, too. I felt the forests of cedars all around my perimeter, their roots reaching down into the damp soil that was also an extension of me. I felt the currents running through me, invisible but tangible, exciting to me, thrilling. I felt the presence of waterfowl bobbing on my surface, diving below now and then to capture small minnows in their beaks. When frightened they rose from my surface; I felt them shove away, then lift, the rhythmic draft of their wings wafting gently over my outer skin. I felt the night air cooling, and saw the mist forming at the coves, rising a few inches from my surface.

The dream took me back to an actual day when I was ten. We had moved from the suburbs of Detroit to a house on a lake sixty miles north of the city. A neighbor had given me an old wooden rowboat with a plank bottom and a pair of very worn oars that rattled in the locks when I rowed. The boat had leaked like a sieve when I first got it, but I had pulled it out of the water, turned it upside down, and after letting it dry in the sun for nearly a week had tarred the bottom to seal up the narrow cracks that let in the water. That's the way it was done by everyone I knew who owned a similar boat. Every year after that, I scraped off the previous year's coating, pressed linseed oil caulking into the cracks, then painted the bottom with thick black tar again.

Shabby though it was, I loved that boat. Others noticed only its rotting boards and squeaking oarlocks, but to me that skiff was the fulfillment of my fondest boyhood dreams. The first year I owned it,

I spent hours on the lake rowing. I loved rowing in the evening, particularly when the sun was just setting and there was no one else out on the water. Ours was a secluded lake, with only a dozen or so families who lived there year-round, the rest of them summer residents who came out from the suburbs from June to September to escape the heat. So in the fall and early spring there was solitude.

Out on the lake, alone at night, I felt cradled between earth, water, and sky, and whenever I rowed the private horrors that haunted me on land became part of a world a universe away. Out on the lake, alone at night, the boundaries of my body dissolved. No, in truth, I went deep, deep into the watery depths of infinite consciousness, deep into myself and beyond it, far beyond it. Rowing, I felt every muscle and bone of my body, felt every cell of me strain against the oars, and lost myself, completely, in the wonder of it.

Out on the lake, alone at night, the mystery of it all opened up to me, and I knew the reason for the dream of the boat was to show me this. It was to show me, beyond all reasonable doubt, that the mystery was enough, would never make itself known to us, and so we should give up the effort. Out on the lake, alone at night, it became clear, in the stars, in the space between the stars, and in the endless flowing of water, that it would always be enough to just bask in the mystery. Just bask in it...that was all I would ever want or need.

Four decades later, I still draw from that youthful memory. The lesson in those experiences with my beloved boat went far beyond my understanding at the time. It has taken me a lifetime to even begin to appreciate the meaning, that we are all one, not only humans and all other life but that which we do not ordinarily think of as being sensate, like water and rocks and the sky. Something unknown, something as essential as water, runs through all of us, the mystery that makes it possible not only to experience each other but to be each other.

Many years after I had left home, and many years after that boat of my dreams had rotted into oblivion, I came upon the idea of peak experiences in a book by Abraham Maslow. In it he spoke of how, during moments of the peak experience in our lives, we have the feeling of merging with our surroundings, of being "at one" with the universe. At the same time, we may also be most idiosyncratically ourselves. So, in peak experiences, we apparently confront our most essential selves as we come face to face with a power much greater than ourselves.

Core Concept

If we turn to the most intense experiences of our past — in this case, peak experiences — we find that they bring us alive. As writers, we depend on these experiences to give us our most vivid emotions, images, tensions, and meaning. It is no wonder that the novelists whose works endure and continue to move us even centuries later are often accused of drawing their imagery and their "fictional" situations from real life.

Out of the peak experiences of my own life, particularly the kinds of epiphanies I relate here, there have come, time and time again, imagery and knowledge that I draw upon constantly in my life as a writer. I have come to look upon the memories of such moments as the creative wellsprings for my profession and from which I have drawn much strength in my life in general.

When my father was dying, now nearly twenty years ago, those early experiences on the lake, I believe, formed a guiding dream that would come to serve not only me and my father but the rest of my family as well. The story is worth telling, if only for the rich imagery that guided me through those difficult days of his passing.

I had not been in close communication with my parents for several years when I received a call from my brother that Dad was in the hospital and was very ill. At seventy-nine, he was not expected to survive the cancer that was invading his body.

Shocked by this news, I retreated to my study and after meditating for several minutes recalled a dream I'd recorded in a journal three months before. I went to the journal, opened it to the page in question, and read the following:

I am on a dock at the edge of a lake, a very big lake where I cannot see the other shore. It may be an ocean or perhaps it is a sea that has infinite borders, stretching on forever. It is dusk. I have led my father down a long ramp to a pier, where a boat is waiting. My father is nervous, reluctant to do what he is about to do, but he has screwed up his courage and is doing it anyway. The boat I lead him to is a wooden speedboat but not of any make or design I've ever seen before. The man who owns it is standing on the pier waiting. As we approach, he greets my father and they shake hands. There is an immediate camaraderie established. The boatman expresses a kind of melancholy that I cannot quite identify. He seems aware that this is going to be a difficult trip for my father, that there is a sadness about whatever it is they are embarking on. My father and the boatman turn their attention to the front deck of the boat, which is a beautifully finished mahogany. Since my father is a cabinetmaker, he has a deep appreciation for such work. He and the boatman talk about the wood, how it was finished, etc. The boatman seems very proud and the two of them really get into this exchange of information. Finally the boatman says something to my father and my father turns to me and says it is time for him to go. We hug and kiss goodbye. My father and the other man get into the boat. I help them shove off, and in moments they are moving out over the water toward the east and toward the endless horizon. I stand on the pier watching until I can no longer see them, and I know that I will never see my father again.

When I read the dream, I again recalled the years on the lake when I was a child. The dream clearly reconnected me with that period. But there was also a message here that I had not recognized the night I'd recorded the dream. Not knowing that my father was ill at the time, it had not occurred to me that the image of the strange boat and boatman could also be an archetype, literally the boatman who comes to carry the dying person over to the other side. Knowing now that my father was actually dying, the meaning of the dream struck me to the core. For several minutes the poignancy of the vision left me in a state of shock. And in the next moment I realized that the imagery was rich with other meaning. I was to be the one to lead my father down to the dock and to the awaiting boat.

This dream and happier memories of my early life on the lake mingled together in my mind. For one thing, I took the dream as a message that I was to go and be with my father, and in some way that I had yet to discover, assist him in his passage. I immediately made airline reservations and set out the very next evening to be with him and my family. I found my father in the hospital, very ill and fully conscious for only all too fleeting episodes.

In the days and weeks that ensued, I spent many hours, as did my mother and brothers, sitting at Dad's bedside. I found that when I sat with him and meditated on the dream, I at first saw only an empty dock. The boat wasn't there. Then, the boat began to appear, first on the distant horizon, then clearer and clearer, until one day it was tied to the pier, the boatman beside it, waiting. For two days, I saw my father going down the ramp with me to the pier, then meeting the boatman, just as I'd seen it in the original dream.

On the third day, when I was exhausted and in need of deep rest, my brother drove me to my parents' home. At 3:10 A.M., the hospital called. Dad had passed over silently and effortlessly in his sleep.

I have written of this experience many times, sometimes fictionalizing it for stories, sometimes taking it pretty much as it happened for an article or portion of a chapter. The rich imagery of my original peak experience has guided me not only at those moments of great challenge, such as my father's death, but in shaping and discovering ideas about my relationship to my world, to my craft, and to myself and my loved ones.

Clearly there's a poetry about peak experiences that transports us beyond ourselves, that gives us access to images and knowledge that perhaps go far beyond everyday understanding. At such moments, we are truly launched into the eye of the mystery, where seemingly unlimited resources open up to us. We are never more ourselves than we are at such moments, never larger, yet at those same moments we also confront the smallness of our individual lives. As often as not, peak experiences liberate

All writers, musicians, artists, choreographers/dancers, etc., work with the stuff of their experiences. It's the translation of it, the conversion of it, the shaping of it that makes for the drama.

— Toni Cade Bambara

me from virtually all fear; basking in the mystery, the recognition of the truth that I will one day die, that I will give up this physical existence, no longer scares me. At least not for now.

As I trace the image of me on the lake, I cannot find where it begins, because it stretches far back through my consciousness, perhaps emanating from the Norwegian seafaring genes that came through my mother's father. From as far back as I can remember, I have felt the pull of the sea, longed as a child of six or seven to sit in my own boat on the waves. I must have been eight or nine when I made a boat, crudely hammering together some boards and making a trailer for my bike to haul it down to a narrow creek a half mile from home. This was in the suburbs before we moved to the lake, and I still recall that long, anxious trip through the streets, with the boat slipping off the trailer several times before we arrived. It was a terrible disappointment, as it turned out. The boat sank to the bottom of the creek the instant I slipped it into the water. We came home that day with a tin can full of crawfish that I kept alive in a fish tank for nearly a week.

What becomes clear to me is that our peak experiences are dictated as much from within as from without. Ancient imagery, maybe stretching back for many generations, guided me to the water and to the source of my first boat. The physical experience of rowing on the lake revivified images and sensations that were not of my making — I am convinced of that. And so, our peak experiences are not only the wellsprings of our creative lives, they connect us with the collective consciousness that has no boundaries or limits.

Even Ocean, the Titan lord of the great river that encircled the earth, as the ancients told the myth, began much farther back in time. And Nereus, Old Man of the Sea, whom Hesiod described as completely trustworthy, always revealing the truth, and whose daughters, the Naiads, danced even in the fountains and springs of Mother Earth, spoke to us humans from a place more ancient.

The dream of the boatman told me I was to become my father's guide in his passing. The Roman poet Virgil, describing the geography of the underworld, told of Acheron, the river of woe, merging with Cocytus, the river of lamentation, both traveled on the journey of our souls out of this life and into the next. He told of the aging boatman named Charon, who ferried souls of the dead over the water to the farther bank, where they are judged and either condemned to eternal torment or blessed and sent to the blissful Elysian Fields. Water runs through our veins, extending far, far back. I have an idea that what we draw upon today is timeless, stretching not only around the earth but as far back as the Word itself, from which God made the world.

If all this is true, and I believe it is, our peak experiences connect us with the original Creative Force. In a hundred lifetimes of the most prolific literary outpouring, we could never exhaust this limitless supply. How odd it seems that such a universal and timeless source could also connect us so unequivocally with our most individual identities!

WRITING EXPLORATION #8
DESCRIBE A PEAK EXPERIENCE

Regardless of the subject we are writing about or the form we use — fiction, nonfiction, poetry, or drama — our voice gives the work its power and its uniqueness. But where do we find this voice? Great writers and storytellers since the beginning of time have known the answer: We discover our own voice when we dare to draw from our own life experience. This is another way of saying, "Write what you know best."

This doesn't mean that all writing is autobiographical, that each character represents something about ourselves or about a real person in our life. And it certainly doesn't mean that every situation we write about is a real event that happened to us. However, the tensions, fears, joys, and sorrows that give our writing its authenticity do so because they are drawn from firsthand experience.

Most mystery writers have never murdered anyone, nor have they known anyone who did. But they do know what it is like to be so angry that they want to hurt someone, and they probably know the grief of losing a person close to them. They build on this knowledge and expand it into more dramatic scenes in their books. Similarly, the person who writes a nonfiction book about an astronaut may never have been to outer space but they have always dreamed of doing so and have imagined what it would be like. That, along with some research, can be a powerful asset for any writer.

What all this means is that we get in touch with our own voice by looking at the experiences that have had the greatest emotional or intellectual impact on us. These may be painful, bewildering, or triumphant. Start now by writing about peak experiences in your own life.

Recall a moment in your past when you felt totally and fully engaged in what you were doing, so thoroughly engaged that you lost your sense of time and felt completely at one with the experience. This could be anything from walking in the moonlight with a lover to a great personal achievement such as writing a book, performing at a concert, completing a difficult assignment, or overcoming a personal handicap. Don't overlook everyday experiences such as gardening, cooking a delicious meal, or making something in your workshop or studio, where you felt a high level of personal involvement and satisfaction. Life's "simple pleasures" have a power all their own that sometimes tell more about life than all our greatest philosophers do.

Write about this experience in the best way that you can, using all your skills to immerse a potential reader in the writing. Then, if possible, read the piece to someone and ask them for their reactions.

Think about ways that you might use this experience in writing an article, story, poem, or book. What might it tell you about human nature? What are the universal themes, such as the joy of accomplishment or the discovery of personal strength, that it reveals? Brainstorm ways that you might use this peak experience as the cornerstone for an article, book, poem, or other item you might write.

CHAPTER NINE

Higher Creativity and the Essential Wound

Well, mythology tells us that where you stumble, there your treasure is....
The world is a match for us and we're a match for the world.
And where it seems most challenging lies the greatest invitation
to find deeper and greater powers in ourselves.

— Joseph Campbell

I don't believe you have to suffer to be a good writer. But I suspect that if you come through life unscathed, you also come through without much of a story to tell. Consider all the effort and self-control it would require to completely escape all pain and travail. Caution like that would be a full-time job, leaving little opportunity, or maybe even energy, for the demands of just plain living, much less writing. Fortunately, few of us have to worry much about this. Besides, it's been my experience that writers in particular aren't richly endowed with the good-sense gene that keeps more sober types out of trouble.

As for the question about how much trouble is necessary, I

can't really say. But too much angst saps your creative juices, and too little turns them rancid. Most writers I know do their best when the hard times are safely behind them. In this respect, it's probably safe to say that no creative muse is worth its salt if it doesn't offer the power of reflection and twenty-twenty hindsight. Without that, we'd have to look elsewhere for the detachment required to work with the really tough material.

There is tremendous energy around our personal travails and woes, and we'd be fools not to tap its creative potential. When I think about the literature that has really moved me, it's often been written by people who dared to look into the shadows where most of us manage to shove the stuff that's too shameful or scary. I think about something Franz Kafka once said: "There are many possibilities before me, but under which rock do they lie?" A friend of mine who writes poetry told me that quote, then added, "You know, I always picture being out for a walk in the woods when I come upon this damp, glistening rock, lift it up, turn it over, and there reaching out to me, clamoring to escape the light, are a million squirming centipedes, a whole world of spiny legs protruding from these dark, writhing bodies."

I may be wrong but it's my belief that all writers write in an effort to heal something in their lives, although I suspect that's why most people do whatever it is they do. Writers and people in the arts are just a little more obvious about it. A lot of what we have to learn in this craft has to do with what we say about our wounds. When I was a teenager, I pored over the novels of William Faulkner, and

I have little doubt that I am still guided — perhaps hypnotized — by what I learned from him. When he talked about writing, he insisted that to be really good writers we must draw creative inspiration from our life experience and that will give depth to whatever we have to say. And above all, he knew that it was from our wounds that we often learned the most valuable lessons, the ones we could pass on to others through our writing.

In December 1950, Faulkner was awarded the Nobel Prize for literature. For years I had a tape recording of the acceptance speech he gave, which I listened to whenever I needed some encouragement in my own writing. In that address, he described what he thought were the responsibilities of the writer in modern life:

> He [the writer] must teach himself that the basest of all things is to be afraid; and teaching himself that, forget it forever, leaving no room in his workshop for anything but the old verities and truths of the heart, the old universal truths lacking which any story is ephemeral and doomed — love and honor and pity and pride and compassion and sacrifice.

Ruminating on those words, I asked what it was about fear that made this worthy of the writer's efforts. And it also suggested to me that there was something to be gained by taking what we have discovered in the best and worst moments of our lives and somehow universalizing them so that they might have meaning for other people.

*The real stuff
of life was
experience, in
which sorrow
and fear and
disaster had as
important a part
to play as
beauty and joy.*

— Sheila Kaye-Smith

Our greatest fears, I believe, don't come from the fear of physical threat or even death but from something deeper than that. Our fear grows out of the dread of not being able to trust our own perceptions about the way the world works. In exactly that vein, my mother was fond of telling a story about me when I was about four years old. A playmate and I had watched our cat giving birth to four kittens. It was a frightening but magical moment for both of us. After it was all done, my friend and I sat down on the back porch of my parents' house and talked about what had happened. According to my mother, my little friend said, "Humans get born the same way, you know. They come out of the mother's body." And I stood up and, with my hands placed stubbornly on my hips, said, "They do not! They come from the hospital."

While my mother always told this as a "cute story" about my growing up, I think I always recognized that something more important had happened to me that day. The little four-year-old had created a reality in his own mind based on humans coming from hospitals. In my innocence, I had put together a limited picture of the world — at least where birth was concerned — based on the scant information that would have filtered down to me at that age. There was probably a certain amount of denial, based on the fact that it was just too preposterous to think that humans would really have to go through the pain and indignity of all that spilt blood, piss, and bodily fluids.

However you look at it, my discovery of the real birth process that day shattered a model of life that I'd held in my mind up to then. And that shattering is always both a wound and a terrible awakening. We're reminded at such times that what we believe isn't always what really is. We'd be fools to claim there's not a certain panic about this — particularly if you don't at least entertain the possibility that there's a power greater than yourself. Life is filled with such moments, of course, with the truth constantly poking fun at our efforts to understand our lives. As the saying goes, "If you really want to make God laugh, tell her your plans."

We make sense of the world through creating these inner pictures of what our lives are about. Most of the time this picture more or less works, so most of the time we're somewhat justified in believing in it. We come to depend on it. Then something happens that pushes the limits, reminding us that we have fabricated these pictures out of our limited view of what makes the universe tick. What's more, we can't always depend on other people — even our loved ones — to comfort or protect us, or even see our needs, when that inner picture fails us.

These essential wounds are at the core of our humanness.

They occur when we confront the outer limits of our abilities, that is, the limits of that inner vision we've constructed of the world from the vast accumulation of our life experiences. We find at such times that life itself is always greater, more expansive, richer, at one and the same time simpler and more complex than anything we can ever hold in our minds. To tell the story of those moments when we've suffered and then healed our essential wounds is to reveal a universal insight that extends far beyond the particulars.

It's difficult to pick out just one example of an essential wound from the myriad of stories that have come out of my writing classes, but I think of the man in his early forties who came up to me after I'd assigned the group to write a short piece about their essential wounds. Barry, I'll call him, said there was something he wanted to write but he could not guarantee that he could finish it, and if I wanted him to read it to the class he was afraid he might not be able to do that, either.

Thinking he was overdramatizing, I told him to just do his best and assured him that I would not force him to read his piece to the class. He

Each sentence must have, at its heart, a little spark of fire, and this, whatever the risk, the novelist must pluck with his own hands from the blaze.

— Virginia Woolf

did not want to tell me what his wound was, but he thought he would tell me the next day, whether he read or not.

I was surprised when we got together the following day that Barry was the first to announce that he would like to read his piece. His voice trembled as he prefaced his story with a description of his father who, he said, figured into his story in a way he had never been quite able to fit in.

"My dad," he said, "was in the Korean War, and when he came back he was without his right leg. He would never talk about what happened and whenever anyone in the family brought it up, he became very agitated, told everyone to shut up, and often vacated the room. The only thing he ever said about the war was that it was in the past and there was nothing to be gained by talking about it. He went on to become a very successful businessman and, I suppose, a good father."

With this preface, Barry went on to read what he'd written. He kept his head bowed as he read, never looking up and never making eye contact with anyone in the room. The piece started out when he was a freshman at a college in the Midwest. It was a beautiful, sunny day, and he was walking across campus with some friends. There had been antiwar demonstrations for the past couple of days, and another rally that afternoon. Suddenly, he thought he heard a car backfire, but the sounds had come from the center of campus, where there were no streets. Several more reports rang out and then he realized that he was hearing gunshots.

For some reason, he raced toward the sound, rather than away from it. As he came around the corner of one of the buildings, he saw the crowd gathered on the lawn. There were soldiers from the National Guard standing off a few yards with their guns drawn. He remembered thinking that they looked like pretend soldiers, young men like himself dressed up in uniforms and carrying weapons.

Someone he barely knew grabbed him by the arm and pulled him through the crowd, jabbering away that Barry's friend had been shot. And then he remembered dropping down on one knee by the limp body of the young man who'd been his friend, and a young woman, a girl in her teens, screaming at the soldiers and holding the young man's head in her lap. The place was Kent State.

As Barry read his piece to the writing class, he broke down and wept several times. But each time he rallied his courage once again and went on.

> After the ambulances came and went, I found myself back at the campus center. I remember there were huge lines at the telephone booths,

Sometimes a person has to go back, really back — to have a sense, an understanding of all that's gone to make them — before they can go forward.

— Paule Marshall

where weeping students were calling their families at home to tell them what had happened and to assure them they were okay. Reporters from the newspapers were already milling around, as were the television cameras. I waited in line for nearly an hour, trying to believe and not believe what was happening. I needed to talk to someone, to try and tell them what was going on with me and maybe get plugged back into a reality I could trust again. When it came my turn to use the phone, I called my dad at his work. He had always been my source of strength when I was a kid. I really looked up to him.

"He's in a meeting," his secretary told me.

"It's important," I told her. "You'll have to interrupt him."

I waited for about five long minutes, and finally my dad got on the line.

"Something terrible has happened," I told him. "I had to talk to you."

He asked me to make it brief because he was in an important meeting. I described what had happened. There was only silence on the line for a long time. I said, "Dad, did you hear me?"

"Yes, I heard you," he replied, his voice cold, more detached and distant than I ever remembered him being. And then, "You're okay? You're safe?"

"I think so," I told him. "I wasn't shot or anything."

"Good," he said. Then, "I have to get back to my meeting."

And that was it! I stood there in the cramped phone booth, holding the dead receiver in my hand and feeling empty and confused.

The horror of the Kent State killings was a big enough wound to last anyone a lifetime. No one in the class would have questioned that. After all, how could any of us create an inner vision of a world where innocents could be shot down in cold blood? But Barry wasn't finished with his story. He went on to describe how the memory of that day replayed over and over again in his dreams, year after year. He had never felt safe after that, though he'd learn to walk down a street with his fear and not cave in every time he heard a car backfire or a sudden sound that he couldn't identify.

The real wound for me wasn't in what the soldiers did that day. I've been over that a million times in my mind. There were crisis counselors to help us after it happened, and I've spent years in therapy. But talking about the soldiers and the killing doesn't help any more. In fact it never did. Every time I think about it, I remind myself that there are thousands of people in the world who see things like that happen every day, and they live with it. Why can't I?

Andrea, a woman in her late seventies, was attending the workshop that day. She'd been very reserved through the previous four sessions, and I'd begun to wonder if she was getting anything at all from the class. So I was surprised when she was the first to speak up.

"Barry," she said, "your essential wound was that your father dropped the ball. You know what I mean, don't you?"

Barry stared across the room at her, and his eyes filled with tears. He could only nod.

"I've never witnessed anything that horrifying," Andrea continued. "But your courage to tell us that story has been very healing for me. We're always dropping the ball, all of us, or we're having it dropped on us. We want so much to believe that we will support each other in times of crisis — but the truth is we often don't. It's not that we don't care or that we're withholding. It's that we can't. Something has happened in our own past that we don't dare look at. We don't know how. We're too busy pushing back our own grief and terror."

She went on to say that Barry's story about his father's wound, with which he had prefaced his story about the shooting at Kent State, reminded her that our weaknesses and faults as human beings often have a long history over which we have little control. She said, "Your father couldn't quite break free of his own history and what he didn't want to talk about. To give you what you needed that day, he would have had to face his own fear and grief and maybe his shame, and he could not do that. But you broke the chain and escaped from your history and his when you had the courage to tell us this story." She paused, seemed to be thinking about what she'd just said, then added: "Your telling this story has helped me to heal. I want you to know that. You didn't drop the ball, and I want to thank you for that."

I'm not sure I understood everything that happened in the workshop that day. But with hindsight, it has become a model for me of why we write, of why we bother with the often painful task of putting our stories down on paper. Each time I think about Barry's story, I'm reminded once again that the story, poem, or book we write isn't the real end product. Our writing isn't finished until it's read. In that respect, Andrea was the quintessential reader that day, revealing that sometimes, when we can summon up the guts to begin telling our truth, the effect ripples out into other people's lives in ways that are as unpredictable as they are courageous. And it becomes part of an evolving consciousness that maybe someday will allow all of us to embrace all of life, to no longer block out what is painful or distasteful. Stories like this are proof that we truly do build bridges between our own consciousness and others' at those moments. Certainly there was a very powerful bridge built that day between Barry, Andrea, and others in the class.

She saw now that the strong impulses which had once wrecked her happiness were the forces that had enabled her to rebuild her life out of the ruins.

— Ellen Glasgow

While all of us experience many essential wounds throughout our lives, usually one or two are pivotal. Earlier in this book, I briefly mentioned a motorcycle accident I had that became a turning point for me. So much came out of that near-fatal event that I have to look upon it with gratitude rather than regret or bitterness. When I look back on it, it seems to me that my life before the accident was chaotic and murky, driven by a strange combination of naïveté, arrogance, and downright confusion. Following the accident, there was a clarity I'd never before known.

At the time it happened, I had recently completed my college education, my son was going on two years of age, and I was beginning to get my writing published. Yet, my life was crumbling around me. Earlier in the year, my wife and I had decided to get a divorce. We hadn't filed any papers yet but it was clear to us both that we would be doing that soon. We were still in that painfully befuddling place that every divorced person knows only too well — when every moment you are apart convinces you your divorce would be the worst mistake you'd ever made in your life, and every moment together convinces you that you can't end this bond soon enough.

My wife and I had made a date to meet that day at the park near where my son and she were living at the time, up on Potrero Hill in San Francisco. I was living across town, renting a gloomy little room from a young couple on lower Nob Hill. Somehow, my wife and I got our signals crossed and she never showed up for our appointment. I was furious with her, disappointed that I would not see my son, and certain she had deliberately not shown up just to punish me. (It turned out I was the one who'd mixed up the date.)

After waiting for more than an hour, I jumped on my motorcycle and took off, determined to immediately go to a lawyer and get the whole nightmare over with. It was a gray, overcast day in San Francisco, and the traffic was light as I approached the stoplight at Twenty-third Street and Potrero. I was driving along at fifteen or twenty miles an hour when the car, a heaving old Pontiac, careened around the corner from Potrero Avenue. He swerved over to my side of the road. I glanced to the left, looking for an escape route, saw the space I needed but hesitated, angry, stubbornly willing the car out of my path.... The next moment I was in the air, flying over the hood of the car.

I vividly remember seeing the driver's face as I hurtled past. He appeared to be laughing maniacally, although I would later learn that he was as horror-stricken as I was. In the next second I was lying on my back in the street. I did not even make an effort to get up. The only sensation I could identify was pain and there was not a grain of doubt that I was badly injured.

Two years before that, I'd learned to meditate and had used this skill for everything from passing difficult tests in school to handling anger. As I lay in the street racked in pain, I began counting my breaths and focusing on a Zen koan I'd been taught. And in the process I calmed myself down enough to assess my injuries. I was pretty certain my left hip was broken, in part because of the pain and in part because that's where the left front fender of the car had hit me. Also, each painfully shallow breath I took convinced me that

I had a number of broken ribs. As near as I could determine, I was not bleeding anywhere. And because I could see, hear, and think pretty clearly, I was relatively sure I didn't have any head injuries.

Two men leaned over me and tried to take hold of my shoulders, talking excitedly in Spanish. When I saw what they were doing — they wanted to get me to my feet — I started cursing them, and between gritted teeth I informed them that if they put a hand on me, I'd kill them. It didn't seem odd at the time, but later when I thought about that scenario I couldn't help but find it a little amusing. Here I was, lying flat on my back in the middle of the street, unable to lift a finger, threatening the lives of two healthy men standing over me — and they were backing away from me as if I was leveling a loaded gun at them!

The next thing I remember was this sweet little old lady bending over me and offering me my glasses, which she'd found lying on the street, I suppose. I smiled as best I could and took them from her. They were nothing but a mangled twist of wire, with both lenses knocked out. I thanked her.

"Can you get me a blanket?" I asked.

I closed my eyes and moments later felt someone covering me with a scratchy blanket that smelled of motor oil. I didn't see who it was that covered me but I gratefully thanked them.

Moments later, the ambulance arrived and after a brief but agonizing ride to the emergency room, I found myself surrounded by the frenetic activity of the doctors and nurses as they worked over me. I'd been taken to San Francisco General Hospital. After all, the accident had occurred practically at their doorstep. For the next couple of hours, I was probed, prodded, x-rayed, and catheterized. Tubes were pushed up my nose, an IV installed, and then a screw was bored through my shinbone with what looked exactly like a carpenter's hand drive. After that, a traction weight was strung from a rack over my bed, attached by a series of ropes and pulleys to the shiny bolt in my shinbone, and I was wheeled onto a ward with thirty-five other men waiting for their broken bones to heal.

At last it was quiet. A doctor and nurse came to my bedside, asked me some questions, wrote down some notes on a clipboard, then gave me a shot of something that burned like fire in my right buttock. I remember asking how long I'd have to stay in the hospital like this, with my leg attached to the bed. The doctor shrugged. "Six weeks or so if everything goes okay," he said.

Before I could recover from the shock of the doctor's announcement, he had turned away and was gone. I felt thoroughly abandoned, confused, and angry. I wanted to scream out to them — to someone, anyone! — to have one human being sit down and calmly tell me, in plain language, what was going on. Then, within minutes, I really didn't care anymore. Whatever the doctor shot into my body was taking effect. I felt warm and safe, secure and loved. I imagined that the vast groaning ward of injured men were all my friends and I was a kid away at summer camp, looking forward to a long, blissful vacation. At last I slipped off to sleep.

Six weeks is a long time to be flat on one's back, totally dependent on others for your most basic needs, with little capacity for anything but reading, talking to people in the neighboring beds, brooding over your fate, or thinking. I had visits from friends, which helped break up the day. One of those visitors was my estranged wife who became perhaps my most important link with the outside world. Two days after the accident, she opened the drawer in my bedside table to get something out for me and noticed my wristwatch. She looked down at the shattered crystal and noted the time the mangled hands were trying to indicate.

"Did this stop when you were hit?"

"Yes," I said. The crystal was pressed against the hands and there was a large dent in the case indicating quite clearly that it would never run again.

"It says 4:20," she said. "I have to tell you something. We were across the bay in Berkeley about that time, at Quentin's birthday party. Nathan was playing, and then he suddenly stopped and went over to the chair where I was sitting and wanted to be held. He became very depressed, and when I asked him what was wrong he said, 'Man crashed. Man hurt!'" He'd repeated it several times.

She couldn't make any sense of this at the time, not knowing about the accident yet. But about a half hour later, Nathan still hadn't come out of his funk so she started making plans to go home. They left the party early, around an hour later, and got home about forty-five minutes later, or approximately 6:00 P.M.

Had it been a mere coincidence that Nathan had made the remark about the man getting hurt at about the same time that I got hit? I didn't know how to answer that, but I did know that the bond between my son and me had always been unusually strong. The possibility that our link might be such that he would have sensed my trouble from thirty miles away moved me deeply. What pained me almost as much as my broken bones was the realization that if this mystical bond with my son was real, it meant he might literally have to share my suffering.

After his mother left that night, I spent a lot of time thinking about that connection between my son and me. I really didn't want to believe it was real. I remembered hearing about such things, but I had never had this kind of apparent confirmation. I'd read C. G. Jung in college a couple years before and remembered his work on "synchronicity," or what he called "acausal relationships" between life events. Jung had told the story of waking up in the middle of the night feeling that someone had entered the hotel room where he was staying at the time. He'd gotten up and turned on a light just to make certain that no one was there. There wasn't, of course, and the door was securely locked. When Jung returned to the bed, he had a pain in the back of his mouth and the back of his head, neither of which were familiar complaints to him.

Because of the strange occurrence, he noted the time and wrote it down in a journal at his bedside. After a restless night he awoke, and when he went down for breakfast he was handed a telegram. A patient of his, living in a city a considerable distance away, had committed suicide during the night by putting a gun in his mouth and pulling the trigger. He had died within minutes of the time Dr. Jung had awakened and experienced the pain.

If one really could sense another's distress across the miles, it meant that perhaps a mystical connection between loved ones transcended the boundaries of time and space. A prisoner of my bed, I had a lot of time to contemplate such things, and from that vantage point I became more and more intent on asking some pretty essential questions.

I noticed, for example, that all the distress I had been feeling about my impending divorce had almost magically dissolved. I recognized that this final separation was inevitable and saw myself carrying through everything necessary to complete it. The terrible angst I'd felt about the breakup, and in particular, my separation from my young son, seemed to lift. The sobering experience of having one's very life threatened, as mine had been by the accident, caused me to see my emotions in a brand-new light.

Core Concept

The writer, like the shaman storyteller of ancient times, embraces his own life experience, tells stories to the community that gathers in a circle around him, a fire blazing at its center. In the telling of what most deeply touched his life, he helps others to see that they are not alone. And in the process both storyteller and listeners are healed.

Strangely enough, this wound was an awakening. For the first time that I could recall, I was able to stand outside myself for long periods of time, to fully participate in my life but at the same time have a new detachment, a consciousness about what I was doing. In a dream one night, I sharply focused on what my distress about the divorce was about. I had loved my son's mother passionately. She had seemed to be the fulfillment of a vision that was deeply ingrained in my very being, my perception of perfect love, and I had thoroughly believed that we would be together forever. In spite of help we got from therapists and our own desire to make our marriage work, it didn't. For the year or two before our final separation, I'd asked over and over again, "What went wrong? How could it possibly be that our relationship has gotten so far off track?"

There were answers, of course. There always are. But were they meaningful answers? And what did it matter if they were? It was clear that our marriage was over. I grieved for the destruction of my vision, but more than that I grieved for what I feared the most — my separation from my son. How would all this affect him?

In a dream, however, a very clear voice told me that all I had to do was let go of my old perceptions and I'd discover an entirely new vision of love. But fear stopped me now, although what I feared the most was that I would never trust my passions again. This would be my struggle from this day forward — the danger that I would never again act on anything I felt passionately about. I would be hyper-vigilant, always trying to protect myself from further hurt. My fear was like a rigid sentry guarding the old vision, telling me it was too precious to abandon. The alternative to my fear was to follow my passions in any case, recognizing the risk and doing it anyway. But first I had to empty myself, to let go of the vision I cherished, and this was hard. It was as if I'd been given this puzzle to solve, with all the pieces neatly laid out for me and crystal clear, but with the solution to the puzzle constantly eluding me. And strangely enough there was something remarkably familiar about the whole thing, an old theme that I'd never been able to get fully in focus.

In any case, that was one of many gifts that came out of that wound. Another had to do with a sense of separation I'd always felt from other people. Since early childhood, I'd always had the impression that my whole life had been a mistake, that I'd somehow been delivered to the wrong parents at a wrong time in history, or that maybe there had been a real screwup and I'd ended up on the wrong planet. I'd always had this sense of being "special," not necessarily in a wonderful way, the way a parent says their child is very special, but special in a sense that made it practically impossible for me to feel a connection with other people.

The wonderful thing about books is that they allow us to enter imaginatively into someone else's life. And when we do that, we learn to sympathize with other people. But the real surprise is that we also learn truths about ourselves, about our own lives, that somehow we hadn't been able to see before.

— Katherine Paterson

In the hospital my specialness was exaggerated all the more because here I was, a nice middle-class young man, with a college education and really nice parents living in the Midwest, tied to a bed in a welfare hospital, surrounded by men whom I never would have otherwise had anything to do with.

In the bed on my right was Percy, a man in his fifties who'd broken half the bones in his body when he fell through a skylight. "I was drunk," he told me. Across the way was Reggie, a black kid of about eighteen who'd been shot in the leg. The gunman had been a shopkeeper on Fillmore Street who caught Reggie breaking in through a rear window. Reggie's femur had been badly shattered but he was just counting his blessings that he was still alive. The shopkeeper had intended to kill him. He had his left wrist handcuffed to the bed because he was under arrest. The cop who guarded him during the day was a young rookie who was pretty nice to him and most of the time treated him like a friend.

About half the ward was black. And from the conversations that went around, I figured that for many of the people there the hospital care they were getting was a lot better than they were otherwise accustomed to.

One afternoon, this wiry black man of about fifty walked over to the side of my bed and started talking. He said his name was Jimmy Gray. I remembered that because I'd had a friend in high school by the same name. He asked what had happened to me, and I told him. Since he was ambulatory, I was curious what he was doing there. He didn't look like he had anything wrong with him.

He said, "They're going to fix my hernia." He admitted he was scared. He'd never had an operation before. He explained that because he was a heroin addict, they couldn't "put me out," so he was going to have the operation with only a local anesthetic.

He told me his whole story, about his operation and his heroin addiction, in an easy, matter-of-fact manner, as I might tell a friend I liked coffee. Clearly things like that weren't big news in his world.

He asked me if I liked the blues. I said I did, and we talked about different blues singers we enjoyed. We both liked Mississippi Fred McDowell, Muddy Waters, Lightnin' Hopkins, and the Chicago blues singers like Jimmy Rush and Joe Williams. He knew a lot of musicians, most of them from New Orleans, people I'd never heard of, and he'd written lyrics for some of them. He asked me if I'd like to hear something he wrote. I said sure. He stood beside my bed, looking out the window, talking his blues like a long poem. The words told about hard times and good times, about falling in love and broken hearts. Sometimes Jesus' name came up. They told about struggling to stay alive when there was nothing to live for, and about friendships that went wrong or that endured the worst kinds of trials. The words told about dreams for a better life, with a sense of hope that defied all reason, given what his life had become.

When he was done, he turned to me and asked how I liked it. I couldn't answer because I was crying. I'm not sure if the tears were because I'd been moved by his lyrics or because they made me feel sorry for myself. He just looked at me and said, "I understand," then patted my shoulder like a caring mother, turned away, and walked out of the room. I never saw him again, though one of the orderlies told me he came through the operation okay and was released, back to the streets, a few days later.

After he left my bedside, I thought a lot about Jimmy Gray, about the lyrics he'd written, and I even entertained the idea of getting him back there so that I could write the words down on paper for him. (He'd told me he couldn't read or write.) But mostly, a passage from the Bible kept coming back to me. Not that I was a great student of the Bible but something had apparently gotten through to me during those years my parents sent me to Presbyterian Sunday school, back in the Midwestern suburb where I grew up. The words I remembered were "Mankind is one." They were words I'd puzzled over for a long time. They'd never made sense to me. That day they did. Because this broken-down blues man's lyrics had revealed to me that in spite of the great gaps that our different ethnic backgrounds created, and in spite of the fact that I had a college education and he couldn't even write, and in spite of the vast chasm between our socioeconomic potentials, we had a great deal in common. We both suffered the same heartaches and celebrated the same joys. We both reached out for hope. Somewhere behind the obvious masks of our differences, we were one.

In the weeks following this encounter, the old sense of loneliness, of specialness, of not belonging dissolved. For the first time in my life I felt that I belonged, that there was a basic truth in this biblical passage — mankind is one — that could not be denied. It was a liberation for me, a casting off of a self-imposed shell that insulated me from the world. Instead of wanting to keep my distance from the other men on the ward, I felt a desire to somehow serve them. In the weeks ahead, I sometimes read aloud to the man in the next bed, who could not read, although he got letters every week from his daughter in another state. It got around that I was writing letters for other people, so I'd get requests from other people on the ward to write notes for them when for one reason or another they couldn't do it themselves.

It felt good to serve others, even in these small ways. When you are bedridden, it is all too easy to feel both helpless and useless, and these little tasks helped to keep me sane. But much more than that, experiencing myself as joined with the others ultimately opened a doorway for me to a kind of love I had never known, although it would take several years for me to really begin to get what that was all about.

During my hospital stay, I observed everything that went on around me. I saw the medical system from the inside out. At some point, I noticed that most people who came into this place totally surrendered to the process. They did not have enough information about medicine or their own bodies to even know what to ask the doctors, so they often abandoned themselves and submitted to treatment that they not only didn't need but that was sometimes downright detrimental — even fatal. After all, welfare hospitals are where doctors learn about medicine. They have to learn some-where! By the time I was dismissed from the hospital, I had inher-ited a mission, to write a book that would demystify medicine and give people information so they could take more responsibility for their health.

It took me nearly ten years to put that book together, but I did it, with the help of my writing partner, Mike Samuels, who also happened to be a medical doctor. The book was published in 1971, one of the first of the so-called holistic health books that would help launch a whole wave of new medical literature for the layperson. Over the ten years it stayed in print, *The Well Body Book* sold more than a quarter of a million copies, in several languages. To this day, I still meet people who haul out old dog-eared copies of that book and tell me stories of how it was their constant companion through the years — *the* book they always turned to when the kids got sniffles or someone showed up with a strange rash. The book would probably never have been written except for that accident and my two-month "residency" at San Francisco General.

The accident that day, and the events leading up to it, literally tore me out of the life I'd known until that moment and offered me the gift of a new perspective, far broader and richer than anything I'd ever imagined. It was not even that it showed me a new way to live so much as it showed me that perhaps I had a choice about how to live. I could, in effect, let go of my old way of looking at the world, knowing there were options, and begin creating a life for myself instead of having it just happen to me. Certainly I didn't have all the pieces — far from it! But without a doubt, what I learned from this wound became a great creative source, showing me that life could be approached far more creatively than I'd been taught was possible.

I am convinced that every essential wound, by its very nature, has the potential for opening each of us up to the full potential of our very soul. I do not mean to be Pollyannaish about it, either. It's not a matter of the universe providing us with the challenges we supposedly need for our spiritual growth. I tend to believe in the universe's "benign indifference," as Camus once put it, and that God is something like a courageous and loving parent who gives us all we can take in, then lets us go on to live our lives the best we know how. I think that must have been what Joseph Campbell was talking about, too, in the quote at the start of this chapter — that "the world is a match for us and we're a match for the world. And where it seems most challenging lies the greatest invitation to find deeper and greater powers in ourselves."

Our own perceptions of the world, the inner vision of what we think life is about, gets challenged in every essential wound. Our true creativity comes about when we start trying to sort all that out, asking what the wound mirrors back to us, what it tells us about ourselves, what we need to let go of, and what we need to learn to embrace. When we do that, we take ourselves out of the role of the victim. We see that there's an alternative to the way we ordinarily look upon our grievances — that we can literally mine even our worst errors for the treasures they contain. When we look at our wounds in this way, we invariably discover turning points, break-throughs that carry us beyond the limits of everyday thinking. And like Barry, we can go forth to tell the stories that are truly important to tell, that reveal the hidden truths of our lives and the lives of others, thus building spiritual bridges between our own consciousnesses and theirs.

Where do we begin? How do we start uncovering the treasures in our wounds? We do that by simply mustering up the courage to look at our lives unflinchingly. After that, the answers always come in a great rush, fueling the creative fires without which a writer is little more than a typist with an attitude.

I can think of no better way to end this, the longest chapter in the book, than with the following quote from a book entitled *Here All Dwell Free* by Gertrud Mueller Nelson:

> Our responsibility, then, is to find and know the story that is our own. We then reach out to grapple with it, choosing to suffer the conflicts that pull us back into our fate and forward to our true selves. As we become healed and autonomous, we reenter our community and our history, offering our gifts to benefit all and taking our place as cocreators of our personal and communal destinies. All three of these tasks, though developmental in nature, are not necessarily done in stair-step order, but cycle around and around, deeper and deeper, as we grow in consciousness and responsibility....Only where we allow ourselves to be fully human can God meet us, and here we encounter our true selves, as if for the first time. Here all dwell free.

WRITING EXPLORATION #9
DESCRIBE AN ESSENTIAL WOUND

As you have seen in this chapter, the essential wound is a particular kind of experience that happens off and on throughout our lives and goes to the very core of our being. These wounds are important to writers for the same reasons that peak experiences are — they are the resources that lend authenticity to our writing. Essential wounds have an added element in that they reveal our humanness. They reveal that we each create our own inner worlds, mental models of the way we believe things should be. The wound occurs when something happens to reveal the difference between how you see the world and the way the world really is. You may feel shattered, hurt, disappointed, or depressed, but if you keep your eyes open those moments can lead to dramatic revelations.

Essential wounds are nearly always pivotal points in the creative person's life because they can cause us to question our personal truths or the personal truths of someone else. We wake up one day, look in the mirror, and discover that we are looking at a stranger. Or we look across the breakfast table and discover that the person we've been married to for twenty years is not at all who we thought they were. Unless we simply block these moments out, they nearly always trigger change. And if you look very carefully at some of the world's greatest writing, you will likely discover the author was motivated by an essential wound.

The assignment now is to write about a moment in your life when you discovered that the world did not conform to the inner vision you had of it. This can be an experience as seemingly mundane as having your fifth-grade teacher criticize a poem you wrote to losing a loved one in a terrible accident. Again, use all your writing skills to render this event as realistically as you can.

When you've completed the writing, read it to a close friend. Ask them how it impacted them emotionally. Then think about ways you might use this experience to reveal something about human nature, personal change, or inner strength, or how to accept defeat and move on to discover a path to greater personal fulfillment. Brainstorm ways you might use your essential wound story to lend your own voice to an article, book, poem, or other item you have either already written or are planning to write.

CHAPTER TEN

Higher Creativity
and the Mask Self

*Where is the I, the entity that decides what to do with
the psychic energy generated by the nervous system?
Where does the captain of the ship, the master of the soul, reside?*

— Mihaly Csikszentmihalyi

I have a friend who's a Catholic priest. Father Sean is a native of
Ireland, speaks with a rich Irish brogue, laughs easily, and
writes wonderful, thought-provoking sermons that sometimes
would make the pope squirm in his seat. A year ago he got his doc-
torate in psychology and has been preparing to take the state
boards to be licensed as a psychotherapist. One Christmas, he
said mass at a small church out in the suburbs. His sermon was
about remembering our true spiritual nature. He started by
describing a trip he'd recently taken to Disneyland, a day before
he was to take the written tests for his boards. He went on all the
rides, then somewhere along the way became fascinated with

the costumed figure of Mickey Mouse that wanders around the park talking to children.

Every time Father Sean turned around, there was Mickey Mouse shaking hands with people, talking with the kids, keeping everyone's spirits up. And Father Sean began asking himself, "I wonder who that person is under that costume? What are they like at the end of the day, when they take off their Mickey Mouse suit?" Having shed their comic book character, how do they treat members of their family, their wife, their kids, the neighbors?

For Father Sean, Mickey Mouse became a metaphor for the way we humans live. Like the person inside the Mickey Mouse suit, we assume a certain character, but soon forget that this "costume" is not our true self. This is not to say that we are like actors, deliberately choosing a certain character to play. On the contrary, we adopt and build that character ourselves, gradually and over a long period of time. Mostly, it happens so gradually that we barely notice what we're doing. By the time we're in high school, we're so deeply identified with this character we literally assume that this is who we are.

I have a friend in New Mexico who tells a wonderful story that I've always liked because it illustrates how these costumes, these Mickey Mouse suits we wear, ultimately become so real to us that we fool even ourselves with them. When she was in her late twenties, my friend went to live on the Zuni Indian reservation, where she had a job as a teacher. As a single mother, she found it to be a nearly ideal place to raise her child. The small-town atmosphere and generally quite loving community provided a quiet, protective environment. Her daughter, blonde and blue-eyed, always stood out in stark contrast to her dark-skinned, brown-eyed playmates, but she got along well with the other children and everyone in the community loved her. One year, when the child was eight years old, she was sitting on a wall in Zuni watching the kachina dances with her little friend, an Indian girl of the same age. Men dressed up in elaborate traditional costumes, each one representing a different spirit or force that exists in the Zuni religion, perform these dances. As the kachinas filed by, the bones and bells attached to their costumes magically jingling and rattling with each dancing step, the Zuni girl turned to her blonde-haired Anglo friend and said, "Do you know the secret of the kachinas?" Entranced by the dancers, her fair-skinned friend shook her head: "No. What is it?" The Zuni girl leaned close and whispered in her friend's ear, "There's really people in there!"

Like the children watching the kachina dances, we easily become so mesmerized by the costumes we wear that we finally come to believe they are the real thing. And to rediscover that there is something more under there that the costume is covering up comes as a kind of revelation. It's all too easy to forget that we didn't come into life with our Mickey Mouse suits on, that we in fact came in as spiritual beings. Father Sean's point was that our life spirit slips into its physical body, taking up residence in that form in much the same way that a person playing Mickey Mouse slips into the costume upon arriving for work at Disneyland every morning.

First, there is the person one thinks he is and the appearance one thinks he has. Then there is the thing one actually is, and there is that which the others think, and here a myriad-faced being arose in her thought, but the second came back as being more difficult to know, for what eyes would see it and where would it stay?

— Elizabeth Madox
Roberts

Father Sean's Mickey Mouse metaphor is very close to what I call the Mask Self. But for me the Mask Self is not a ready-made character that we arbitrarily assume. Rather, it is something that we ourselves mold and create, although we do so on a more or less unconscious level. In effect, the Mask Self is the product of our own life experiences, the lessons we've learned along the way through our essential wounds and our peak experiences. The Mask Self is the self we have constructed to feel safe in the world. In many ways it functions as a shield, protecting our vulnerable inner self from the "slings and arrows" of the outer world.

THEATER AND ITS DOUBLE

Years ago, I spent a lot of time with avant-garde theater groups in San Francisco who were experimenting with the use of masks in performance. I became fascinated by what happens to both actor and audience when a person dons a mask. It is as if the mask takes over, dominating the actor. The best masks depict a certain character even before the actor puts it on, and once in place over the actor's face, the mask tends to dictate what the actor will say, how he or she will move; it even gets the actor thinking and responding to other actors in a certain way.

As spectators, we tend to forget the actor under the mask and respond instead to the mask. If you've ever seen a group of children watching a puppet show (the puppet being another kind of mask), you'll recognize how thoroughly convincing a mask can be. When my son was still very small, he had a collection of hand puppets he played with; when I put a puppet over my hand, disguised my voice, and talked to Nathan, he would carry on long conversations with the puppet, as if I wasn't even there. I noticed the same thing with other children when Nathan's friends came over to the house to play. When the kids spoke with the puppets, they also took on "disguised" voices, just as I did when I worked the puppets. To me this meant that at some level the children knowingly participated in the puppets' fantasy world, not unlike what we all do with the Mask Self. We instinctively know there is a truth beyond the mask but we willingly participate in maintaining the illusion that this is all there is.

One of the theater groups I worked with performed in the tradition of commedia dell'arte, a theater form that was popular throughout Europe during the Middle Ages. Usually, these performances were given in public places, such as open-air markets or festivals. And as often as not, the plays had a set story line within which the actors improvised their individual lines. Sometimes they carried an underlying political message, everything from the age-old sport of lambasting the royalty to advocating revolution. One group I worked with was the San Francisco Mime Troupe, who performed in the parks. This was during the late 1960s and early 1970s, when we had very active civil rights demonstrations and the antiwar movement was growing up. Most of the Mime Troupe's performances dealt with those themes, often in very powerful ways.

In the initial phase of putting a production together, the Mime Troupe's actors worked long hours with their masks and costumes. Many made their own masks or worked closely with the costumer so that a mask eventually came to be a blending of the actor's personality and the character they were to play. Then, at that magic moment when they walked out on the stage, the actors I had known backstage were completely transformed. I no longer saw an actor as the person I'd had dinner with an hour before. It was as if the mask focused on one specific portion of their own character, allowing them to exaggerate some aspect of themselves, ultimately developing it as a full character. At times the transformation would be frightening — as when the person who was a perfect saint offstage became the arch-villain behind his long-nosed black mask and flowing cape. Having assumed the character of the mask, he drew from a dark, shadowy side of his being, bringing it forth in the context of the loosely drawn script.

The years I spent in the theater were really quite wonderful, although looking back on it I realize that it was not the theater itself that interested me so much as what it taught me about our human capacities and the world of illusion that is our daily lives. The recognition that actors could become not just one character but many suggested to me that perhaps behind the Mask Self that we present to the world in our day-to-day lives, we are all many other subcharacters, all of which play important roles in our lives. Unbeknownst to me at the time, each of these revelations about our masks was taking me closer and closer to that truth Father Sean described in his sermon.

Core Concept

Even as conflict rises out of the disparity between the Mask Self and the deeper reality of the inner self, here we may explore what is true and universal, touching all our lives, no matter who we are or what we claim to be.

At approximately the same time that I was working in the theater, I was also taking part in a study on the use of hallucinogens in psychotherapy. One weekend, a Native American peyote shaman introduced a small group of us to this ancient herb and its use in spiritual ritual. After ingesting what looked like small cactus apples, with the foulest taste one could ever imagine, I began to shiver uncontrollably. When the shaking finally settled down, I suddenly became warm and comfortable, almost euphoric, and began having beautiful visions, little bursts of brilliant colors, all in elaborate, geometric shapes, similar to the geometry of snowflakes but with much more color, and with no two ever exactly alike. This shower of colorful shapes was the welcoming celebration for events that were soon to follow.

Immediately after this, I started having vivid waking dreams. I saw beautiful landscapes, houses, the interiors of rooms, and people. At one point, I had to walk out through the darkened rooms of the house where we were staying to go to the bathroom. Along the way, I met several dream-people, stopping to have short conversations with each one. In the dream space the peyote provided, these people seemed no different from people you or I might meet on the street. Although I knew they were dream figures, they always appeared quite autonomous, speaking back, laughing, listening, often in unexpected ways.

By the time I'd returned to the room where the others in our experiment were sitting, I was beginning to feel that all the dream figures I'd met and spoken with seemed familiar to me. Back in the room, I asked the shaman if he knew about such characters. Did they appear in this way for everyone? And who were they, anyhow?

"Are they people you know in real life?" the shaman asked.

"No. Definitely not. Yet, when we speak to each other, I feel the way I do when I am around close friends. We can talk as if we've shared a long history together."

"Then they are from your dream world," he said. "They are the people from your inner world."

"Like characters I have created in my dreams?"

"Not exactly," he said. "In my tradition, it is believed that we take part in two different worlds, the world of dream and the world we most often refer to as reality. But according to our way, only the dream world is real. The reality we call the physical world is the illusion. That's just the opposite of the way most people are taught in the schools today. Our task in this life is to learn from the inner world and to understand how these two worlds can help each other."

At the time, I was skeptical about what he had to say. I could buy the idea that at a deep psychological level we might create different characters to represent aspects of ourselves. But the idea that these characters might have lives of their own, separate from us, seemed preposterous.

Following this session, I thought a lot about what the shaman told me. And in the half dozen or so sessions we had after that, I began exploring the dream figures that appeared. The first of these was a woman who I called Alycia. She was in her late forties or early fifties, rather tall and of medium build, with curly salt-and-pepper hair, cropped close to her head, and soft brown eyes that always looked a little worried or distressed. I first saw her as

Dreams are . . .
illustrations
from the book
your soul
is writing
about you.

— Marsha Norman

165

a generous nurturer, a person who was always looking for ways she could help others, a kind of saint. Once I'd made contact with her, I was puzzled by how I felt toward her. Frankly, though she seemed generous, self-effacing, and sincerely helpful to others — including me — I didn't like her. The fact is, I felt threatened by her. In her presence, I became deflated, weak, and resentful. It took me years to discover what that was all about: Her helpfulness was motivated not so much by truly wanting to help others as it was by a driving need to prove that she was a good person.

I wrestled with the image of Alycia for years, sometimes seeing myself doing exactly what she was doing — rescuing people in need to prove that I was good. At other times, I'd find myself drawn to people who, like Alycia, had a need to be helpful, and these relationships always proved disastrous. Then, an odd thing began to happen. Alycia began to change. It was as if she had suddenly seen what was going on in her life, and that some of the work I'd been doing in my life, wrestling with the two sides of the nurturer, was reflecting back to her. Somewhere along the line, we both recognized that we could never find the self-respect and self-love we'd been seeking on the path we'd been following. I began to see that instead of turning to the outside world for support and self-affirmation, I could draw from an inner wisdom that, quite simply, made me feel very good about myself.

As I learned to draw from this place of inner wisdom, the need to prove I was good began to diminish. Although I often found myself lured into the helping role, it was now in a very different light. In my writing and teaching, for example, I began attracting readers and students who had particular skills they wanted to learn. They came for these, rather than to be rescued from themselves. And it was after that subtle but important shift occurred in my life that I learned how teaching and learning can be the same thing — that as teachers we are doubly blessed because we learn at least as much from our students as they learn from us.

Today, whenever I think of Alycia, or she comes up in my dreams, I feel love and admiration for her. She and I have both changed and it is impossible to determine which of us initiated these shifts in our perspectives. The distrust and ambivalence I once felt so strongly toward her are no longer there. It is nice to believe that we two have come a long way together, and we recognize that we, too, have been teachers to each other.

While many other characters inhabit my dream world, I think my relationship with Alycia is probably the best illustration of how we can work with this inner world. I think, for example, that in writing a novel, getting in touch with our personal dream figures becomes

My mind is a world in itself, which I have peopled with my own creatures.

— Lady Caroline Lamb

a key source of our creativity. In nonfiction, I believe that our strug-gles with the issues we have with these dream figures, or their coun-terparts in the external world, provide us with our greatest passions. It's this kind of passion that you need to keep you motivated through the long, tedious task of writing a book. When we're con-nected with these passions, issues such as "disciplining" ourselves to write fall by the wayside. Passion, after all, is its own motivator. Ultimately, the question is no longer how we can discipline our-selves to write, it's more an issue of disciplining ourselves to stop.

Behind the Mask Self we find a myriad of dream figures, per-haps a whole world of them, an entire planet! Just as in our wak-ing lives, some will be more prominent than others. In an entire lifetime, it is impossible to get to them all. But I believe that through the synergy of the inner and outer worlds we lift the mask, ultimately stripping it away enough to catch at least a fleeting glimpse of our souls, our true spiritual nature.

Part of the job of writing is to excite and entertain our readers; but the other part of that job is to establish clearer relationships with the inner world. In any case, I don't think you can really accomplish the first part of this job description without doing the second. Our creative passion comes through as we become fully engaged in this dance between inner and outer, and that passion is what makes our writing electric.

I don't think all writers consciously explore dream time, at least not the way I describe. But there's no doubt in my mind that, conscious or not, we all draw extensively from this source.

THE EVOLUTION OF THE MASK

The Mask Self is that part of ourselves that we dare to present to the world. It is a way of being that we have put together, frequently in a rather haphazard way, and often through the trials and errors of our lives. For the most part, the Mask Self protects us from having to look more closely at the dream figures that lie behind it. It protects the more vulnerable creatures of our inner world.

In an ideal universe, there would be no need for the Mask Self and no need to protect our inner worlds. We would simply come into life, into the arms of loving parents who would take one look at us, and with complete and total awe, exclaim, "My God, what a wonderful creature! I wonder what gifts she is bringing into this world? How can I ever discover what these are, nurture them, and allow her to fully blossom?" But as parents, we're seldom that magnanimous, insightful, or secure in ourselves. Out of our own fears and insecurities, we press in on the infant. Rather than asking how we might nurture this new being so that she can deliver her new gifts to the world, we get overly responsible. We think, "Oh, I must groom and shape this little being into a responsible citizen. I must make certain that she is well disciplined, that she gets a good education so that she can go out and get a good-paying job or meet a rich husband." As well-meaning as these motives might be, the gifts the child is bringing into the world may be completely ignored or shoved aside and that child, in effect, becomes invisible.

Years ago, I spent two weeks in a college course entitled "The

Psychology of Education," in which the instructor said that as infants we come into the world as empty vessels and our task as parents and teachers is to fill those vessels up. I sat through three hours of this instructor's lectures before I walked out, convinced that this approach to education was inherently destructive. I didn't know what offended me so deeply then, but something did, that was for certain. To me an element of this instructor's philosophy was painful and mean, and I found myself reacting way out of proportion to what had been said. But maybe my outrage was justified after all.

I think what I got in touch with that day was a wound most of us suffer when we're growing up — that somehow, in the course of even the most loving parents' efforts to bring us up, who we really are gets ignored. We get wiped out, or nearly so. In our early years, we recognize how dependent we are on the adults in our lives. We need them to feed us, clothe us, shelter us, and give us love. And in our innocence we really don't know how to judge whether the adults in our lives are truly trustworthy. Instead of being who we really can be, we take on masks like the Good Little Girl, the Good Little Boy, or we become the Black Sheep of the Family or the Rebel. There are, of course, a myriad of possibilities. But the point is that early on we learn that if we are to be loved and cared for we'd better buckle under and be what is safe for us to be within the family dynamic.

Once we have the Mask Self set in place, we have our position in the family system staked out. With our Black Sheep mask in place, for example, we become the recipient of all that's wrong with the family. Others don't have to own their dark side because you have been defined as the Black Sheep and will act it out for them. Furthermore, you'll continue to be valued as long as you agree to play that role. As long as you wear your Black Sheep mask, you've got a place in the family.

Eventually there comes the time when you move outside the family unit. Out in the world people have different needs. Not everyone is going to find value in your Black Sheep mask; indeed, they want only to push you away or try to control your behavior. Lovers, teachers, employers, the police will all try to make you over. Most will attempt to train you to be a Good Little Boy instead. Maybe they'll even succeed! Ironically, whether you are success-ful or not, you are still invisible. You still haven't embraced who you really are.

As we struggle with our masks, there are often many different layers to be peeled away. In the meantime, life becomes a melodrama, a soap opera, as we find ourselves drawn to this person or that, all in an effort to make our lives work and still hold onto our masks. For a while

Clarity is the perception of wisdom . . . being able to perceive and understand the illusion, and to let it play. It is being able to see beyond the activities of the personality to the force of the immortal soul.

— Gary Zukav

we may be able to get someone to play the game with us: The person with a Rescuer mask hooks up with the Maiden in Distress mask, the person with a Victim mask hooks up with the Abuser, and so it goes.

Through all these dances, we play out the insanity of our lives. To some degree, I think we have little choice but to do that. Each time we play and lose we're forced to look a little more closely at ourselves, to ask what all our challenges are trying to mirror back to us. And bit by bit we dare to lift a corner of the mask and peek under it. If we're lucky, there are times when we're caught off guard, without our masks, and at those moments of epiphany — through our peak experiences or essential wounds — we perhaps catch a glimpse of a truth bigger than the mask. If we have enough of these, and if we get to the point that we're no longer willing to suffer the perils of wearing the mask, we begin pursuing the larger truth.

The true self behind the mask, and beyond the great cast of characters we call our inner world, knows that our true nature is spiritual and can see beyond the Mickey Mouse suits. The true self knows that beyond the Mask Self that each of us wears in the world, *mankind is one*.

My friend Phil, who is a psychiatrist but also a spiritual teacher, says, "The illusions of separation we experience are only that — illusions. It is impossible not to be *at one*. Whatever we experience to the contrary can only be of our own making."

What I take this to mean is that we create these illusions of separation through our masks, and our life dramas are little more than the playing out of these illusions. Yet, at the same time these dramas are very much a source of our passions and our creativity. We needn't go out looking for anything else to fill the pages of our books. To focus on these personal truths, to dare to look closely at our masks and the inner worlds beneath them, is the way we come back to ourselves, not only to our spiritual essence but to the stories we must live through along the way.

The dramas we play out through our masks are, after all, part of our life history. They make up the legends of our life journey, and certainly the enigma of truth is reflected in them. The masks we wear, the characters we find peopling our inner world, the dramas we play out in the external world — all of these provide us with unlimited themes, anecdotes, and illustrations to say virtually anything we might wish to say — in fiction, nonfiction, poetry, or drama. By using this material, we benefit twice: First, in the passion we bring to our writing, and second, in our discovery of the path back to our true selves.

WRITING EXPLORATION #10
DESCRIBE A MASK UNVEILED

It is often said that nobody can ever know us as well as we can know ourselves. Part of the reason for this is that very early in our lives we learn a way of being that prevents people from seeing our whole self. Here's how it works:

Perhaps we get punished for being too outspoken and so we learn to hold our tongue and be more reserved. Or we learn that our parents are happiest with us when we excel in school subjects that will lead to a college education and a professional career. While we may not completely like how we feel when we are doing these things, we gain a sense of inner security and self-esteem, or perhaps even feel that we are loved, which at least for the moment seems worth the price.

Meanwhile, who we really are — our innate gifts, the activities, and the personal expressions that truly light up our lights — are being ignored or even discouraged. As a result, we develop a mask, a way of being in the world that wins us certain rewards: monetary gain, financial security, a family member's approval, self-esteem for being able to do something well even if you don't like it, or social status within a certain group. But beneath the mask is something more, a self that the rest of the world doesn't see and that is dying to be expressed.

Write about a mask experience. The possibilities are many. For example, write about one or more of the following:

- Feeling that you wanted to be a writer while your parents forced you to go into the family business or encouraged you to become a _____ (you fill in the rest).
- How you discovered that someone close to you was not who they appeared to be, owing to the fact that you were only seeing their mask, not the real person beneath it.
- How you dared to remove your own mask, discovering talents and desires that until that moment you had not dared to express.
- How you were able to confront a personal weakness — maybe an addiction or other destructive personal habit that your mask was covering up. Then tell how by stripping away your mask and looking at your "shadow" you discovered a self that brought you joy and success.
- How you and a close friend, spouse, lover, or family member confronted your respective masks and vastly improved your relationship.

After writing about this mask experience, read it to a friend and ask them how it impacted them. Then think about ways the same event could become the inspiration for writing something that would truly make a positive difference in other people's lives.

CHAPTER ELEVEN

Beyond the Mystic Circle of the Storyteller

The most beautiful thing we can experience is the mysterious. It is the source of all true art and science.

— Albert Einstein

When I was in my late twenties, I spent several months doing dream work with a Freudian psychotherapist. For the first five or six weeks, the work we did was by the book, with the therapist interpreting my dream imagery in a fairly traditional way. Everything I dreamed seemed to symbolize conflicts with my mother or repressed aggression toward my father. While this was interesting, I began to notice something else in my dreams, something beyond the symbolic. As I got into the discipline of keeping a notebook at my bedside and waking up to record my dreams, I noticed that much of the time these nocturnal voyages were like stories. They often had beginnings, middles, and ends. They had integral characters and even, at times, intriguing story lines, plots, or settings.

Core Concept

Dreams and visions are not always intended to be interpreted or analyzed. At times they say exactly what they mean, providing a set of images and meanings to be taken for no more or less than they are. At this point, the writer becomes as much a shaman or prophet as an artist, and one should not shrink from this responsibility.

In one of the first complete dreams I could accurately recall and write down, I was sitting in a theater. There was a round stage in the middle of a round room. The theater was packed, with the audience seated in seven circles of seats around the stage. I sat in the second row in the best section of the audience. It seemed that I was both a spectator and a member of the cast. I had a telephone with which I could be in constant communication with the actors as they played their parts. The actors themselves wore headsets with tiny microphones so that we could talk back and forth as the play was going on. There was a spotlight on me, signaling the audience that I also had a role in the play, though I spoke lines the audience could hear only twice — once at the beginning of the play, when I introduced the actors, and the second time at the end, when I delivered a closing monologue. I remembered the closing line very well, because it was derived from Shakespeare: "We are all like actors, who strut and fret an hour upon the stage and then are heard no more."

The actors on the stage were all very familiar to me, and I recognized that they represented, and were playing out, various parts of myself. They were following a script but while they acted out the scripted story, I would pick up the phone, dial one actor or another, and make suggestions for things they might say or do. Things that happened on the stage triggered spur-of-the-moment innovations, not anything we'd rehearsed or that I'd previously written down. I was always aware of what we'd rehearsed and what was improvised in the moment. To add complexity to the play, the actors spoke in two different languages, both of which the audience understood. There appeared to be one language for symbolic meanings, and another for more literal, everyday messages.

It was an intriguing production. Most of the time, the action unfolding on the stage came as a complete surprise to me. And at other times, when I telephoned an actor and asked them to try something that was not in the script, the unexpected turn of events that resulted would surprise us all. While I only had a vague memory of the basic script, the main story line seemed to be made up of fragments from a variety of Eugene O'Neill's plays, whose work I happened to be reading at the time. As the play ended, the audience applauded, and when I stood up and bowed from my place offstage, the applause rose even higher. I bowed, feeling tremendously satisfied with myself.

In my next therapy session, I brought along my dream journal and read the description of this dream to my therapist, glowing with pride. To my frustration, she looked thoughtful and grave, then spent the next twenty minutes explaining to me that it was all about fear and my need for control. She told me that I was in the audience, as the director of any play might be, but the telephone line to the actors symbolized my unwillingness to let go and trust the actors. The actors, she said, symbolized important people in my life, and she promised that in our next sessions together we could dissect my relationships with them in greater detail.

That night, I sat down and considered what she had told me. I agreed that while the dream probably did reveal something about my need for control, I also saw it as a fascinating concept for a theater piece. Since I was apprenticing in the theater at the time, I began to write a play based on the dream — with an actor in the audience with a phone and others onstage with headsets. Moreover, I devised a way for the actors to turn and speak directly to the audience, while giving the illusion that the other actors couldn't hear them. In a way, then, there were two separate languages represented, one that communicated within the action of the script, the other a private language between certain actors and the audience.

As an artistic piece, the idea was more ambitious than I had the skill to handle at the time, so I eventually shelved it. But what came out of this experience was the realization that our dreams really are a tremendous creative wellspring. There may be layers and layers of symbolic meaning to be mined for psychotherapy, but on a more obvious level we should also learn to appreciate our dreams as, quite literally, creative brainstorms. Since that day, I have always looked to my dreams for ideas that might be developed into stories, articles, new forms, characters, or nonfiction book ideas.

Many years after I'd left psychotherapy, I became interested in shamanism and the use of dance and ritual in early societies. What intrigued me was that shamans often drew their wisdom not only from tradition and direct experience but from what parapsychologists and mystics call the invisible reality. The shaman believes that there is a reality that parallels our physical lives but that we cannot hear, see, smell, taste, or touch. It is a world outside our five senses. Those of us who were raised within the scientific tradition are taught that what we cannot perceive through our senses does not exist. And, of course, there is much debate, even in the scientific community, about this subject.

True shamans live in a world that is alive with what is to rationalist sight unseen, a world pulsing with intelligence.

— Paula Gunn Allen

Within most shamanic traditions, dreamtime is believed to be the way we access the wisdom of the invisible reality. Through active imagination, hallucinogens, ritual, drumming, and dance, the shaman enters an altered state of consciousness. In this state, he or she may see themselves not just as witnesses of their dreams but as participants. And from their journeys in this other world, they bring back visions and teachings to assist their tribes in making changes, be it in finding a new hunting territory, healing a personal relationship, or bringing greater balance and harmony between the tribe and the natural order.

Often, the shaman's wisdom was communicated to others through storytelling. Members of the community would sit around in a circle and the storyteller would get up and tell his or her story, very often acting out various parts, seeming to take on the guise of another person, an animal, or a god. The stories were always seen as coming from the invisible reality. Even when the storyteller repeated one of the more traditional stories, for example, stories of Coyote the Trickster, he or she would put their own spin on it, virtually reinterpreting the old tales every time they were performed.

Although several years passed between the time I had the dream about the theater and the time I became interested in shamanism, I remembered the dream and went back to the journal where I'd recorded it. I was immediately surprised at the similarities between that dream and certain shamanic practices. The first thing that impressed me was the similarity between the theater in the round and the traditional medicine wheel of the indigenous societies. The medicine wheel is, in effect, a group of people gathering in a circle. In the circle each person brings his or her voice to the center, in response to a problem the community may be having. Out of the synergy of the total group's participation comes a new direction or vision of the problem. In that respect, no single person is considered to have the final solution; rather, the group believes that the Great Spirit moves through each person, and each one contributes his or her small piece of the total picture. Only when the total activity of the medicine wheel is viewed as a whole do we have anything resembling an understanding of the issue.

Often, the stories of the shamans or other storytellers, which you'll remember originated in the dream space, would establish the theme, as it were, for the medicine wheel. Ultimately, then, there was complete interaction between any single storyteller and the other people sitting in the circle. The story, drawn from dream time, literally entered the consciousness of the spectators, perhaps triggering ideas or visions that would then be fed back to the circle when those spectators spoke or in some other way

This is what art is all about. It is weaving fabric from the feathers you have plucked from your own breast. But no one must ever see the process — only the finished bolt of goods. They must never suspect that that crimson thread running through the pattern is blood.

— Katherine Paterson

took an active part in the circle. Their actions might be telling another story, dancing, drumming, or simply speaking their mind.

What I began to see was that these early storytellers were deeply involved with the invisible reality — which today would be called our emotional and spiritual life. They saw life as a constant interweaving between the physical world and this other reality that exists outside the reach of the five senses. They believed their work on the physical plane was relatively straightforward, consisting of learning how to feed, clothe, and shelter themselves and their families and developing positive relationships with their community. The more difficult work was encountered in their relationship to the invisible reality, that is, honoring the spiritual life and their relationship to the universe.

As storytellers, then, their work was not aimless recreation but was a way of giving the invisible reality form in the physical world. The story drawn from dream time invariably brought a message that helped storyteller and spectator alike better understand their relationship with the spiritual life. What's perhaps even more important to see is that when these stories were performed, there was very hot participation with the spectator. The storyteller would respond to his listeners, just as any live entertainer responds to his or her audience today. In working together, storyteller and listeners pumped the deep inner wisdom from the conduit the storyteller had set up with the invisible reality.

When the printing press came into widespread use, it created a separation between the writer and the reader (or listener) that was never present in the days of the early storytellers. Today, with the printed word, the author has little or no contact with the reader, and the pump that the synergy between storyteller and listener provided has all but disappeared. After all, readers are not present during the actual performance, that is, the writing, which limits their impact on the creative process. Still, any writer worth his or her salt still draws from the invisible reality — the dreams, the visions, the memories, and the imaginings that come out of our life experience.

The invisible world, the world of imagination and dream, is filled with mystery and rich with creative resources, so as writers we should take advantage of any opportunity to draw from it. To maximize our use, we need to get away from dream interpretation. While I think there is much to learn about our emotions from our dreams, I sense that as writers we make full use of this tremendous resource only when we honor the mystery and allow this other reality to tell us its stories. Instead of attempting to interpret the hidden language of this reality, take the stories and characters whole. Always

There are only two ways to live your life. One is as though nothing is a miracle, the other is as though everything is a miracle.

— Albert Einstein

remember that they are much more than the symbolic interpretations you might impose on them. Play them out on the page by telling a story or following a theme you may have recognized in them. And finally, when you write, pretend you're a storyteller sitting with a group of people around a campfire at night. Imagine the live presentation of your material and its effect on the other people in the circle. Respond to their cheers, their oohs and ahhs by shifting your story slightly, embellishing it here and there for a deeper effect.

As modern writers, it's all too easy to lose sight of the fact that we can and do have an impact on thousands of people. The realities we create on the page enter into the readers' lives, in some cases radically changing them. You would immediately understand this impact if you were working in the oral tradition, telling stories to a circle of your community members; we frequently lose sight of it when we're telling our stories for the printed page. A mystical connection between writer and reader needs to be honored, one that skeptics might challenge but that is increasingly difficult to deny.

As a writer, I have been fascinated by the emerging new sciences that recognize the existence of an invisible reality beyond the reach of our five senses. And it is particularly interesting to note, as Joseph Campbell did, that as technology has evolved to the point of allowing us to send astronauts to outer space, we are awed more than ever by what we find in our voyages beyond the earth's atmosphere. Campbell himself makes the point that "the voyages into outer space turn us back to inner space...."

Brian O'Leary, an astronomer, NASA scientist-astronaut during the Apollo program, and deputy team leader of the Mariner 10 television science team, wrote: "The new reality presumes an interconnectedness, a higher order in the universe that cannot be explained simply by known physical laws. It observes the power of the mind.... It considers dimensions beyond time and space, concepts beyond matter and energy as currently understood, and realms beyond the physical...."

We are not, by any means, the first generation to recognize the existence of this other reality. In the early twentieth century, for example, C. G. Jung explored this reality about as thoroughly and scientifically as anyone has in recent history. In fact, toward the end of his life he attributed much of the success of his intellectual efforts and his writings to experiences he had with inner guides. These were "disembodied entities," which emerged from his deep unconscious mind and provided him with information; the best known of them was Philemon, whose counsel he consistently called upon throughout his life. He described Philemon, in the following way: "Philemon represented superior insight. He was a mysterious figure to me. At times he seemed to me quite real, as if he was a living personality. I went walking up and down the garden with him, and he was what the Indians call a guru."

Jung believed these fantasy figures had an identity separate from his own mind. He stated that his experiences with Philemon and other figures brought home to him the "crucial insight that there are things in the psyche which I do not produce, but which produce themselves and have their own life." He believed, like so many students of the new science, that at least part of the psyche is not subject to what we presently perceive as the limits of time and space. He stated, himself, that "the psyche at times functions outside of the spatio-temporal law of causality. . . ."

In recent years, there has been an increasing interest in channeling, whereby a person makes contact with an entity or disembodied soul from the other side. The best known of these are Jane Roberts's "Seth" channelings, the channeling of *A Course in Miracles* by the psychologist Helen Schucman, and the work of Kevin Ryerson, popularized by Shirley MacLaine. When we look at the writings of these, as well as others, we do find bits of quite extraordinary wisdom, often beyond the range of the channel's own study and education. It seems that regardless of the explanation for this practice, it appears that the authors somehow created what amounts to a psychic conduit from their everyday realities to one that cannot be easily explained in conventional terms.

The practice of creating a certain character unlike ourselves, or of assuming a character from another source, such as a legendary hero or a religious figure, goes as far back in history as we can trace. I mentioned one example of this in the previous chapter, where I told the story about the little girl's remark about the kachina dancers. Most early societies had dances and other ceremonies where a man or woman would don the costume and mask of a deity. In doing so, they literally took on the character of that figure and lost their own identity. Once fully in character, the dancer under the mask seemed to disappear, saying and doing things that appeared to be quite beyond their capacities in their everyday state of mind. This, too, was a form of channeling.

I know of no satisfactory explanation for what happens when we assume characters other than our own and use them as ways of accessing information from other psychic dimensions. Clearly, this experience is a wonderful addition to one's creative process. At the very least, I would have to agree with Arthur Hastings, Ph.D., whose book *With the Tongues of Men and Angels: A Study of Channeling* is without a doubt the most responsible and exhaustive treatment of this phenomenon in print today. In that book he concluded:

> We do not have enough understanding of the mind and its reaches to say with certainty what is possible and what is not. Our beliefs should be open to change as we learn more. We can still come to conclusions for practical purposes and test their value by how useful they are in understanding experience and guiding action. The models we use should be stepping-stones for further exploration.

Techniques for developing these characters vary widely, from immersing yourself in the history of a figure from history, to asking a guide to come to you in your dreams, to entering an altered state through deep meditation from which you simply ask a figure to come to you for help with a specific issue or writing problem. In chapter five, I spoke of a spirit guide of mine named Awahakeewah

We have these instincts which defy all our wisdom and for which we never can frame any laws. . . . They are powers which are imperfectly developed in this life, but one cannot help the thought that the mystery of this world may be the commonplace of the next.

— Sarah Orne Jewett

to whom I often turn for guidance in my writing. That guide came to me initially when I was still in high school. During a hunting trip in northern Michigan, I sat down under a tree, and in the process of trying to make myself comfortable I reached under my right buttock to remove what I thought was a sharp rock. Instead, my hand curled around what turned out to be a beautifully sculpted tomahawk head, several hundred years old.

Some years later, I was holding the tomahawk head in my hand while meditating. As I moved deeper and deeper into this meditation, a figure of an Indian began to form in my mind. It was a vivid image, and like C. G. Jung, I was somewhat startled because he seemed very real to me, not like a character I'd create for a story but much more than that. Awahakeewah explained that he had made the tomahawk head and that he had also been a toolmaker for the community in which he had lived. His lecture to me about the Creative Spirit, which I recorded in chapter five, has continued to have a very strong influence on me, and I often turn to him for guidance whenever I have trouble in that area. My work with that guide has convinced me that there is another dimension of reality, much greater than our firsthand experience of the world. We probably have access to this dimension at all times, although we don't often make use of it in the modern world, where we have learned to discount such beliefs on scientific grounds.

Jon Klimo, interdisciplinary researcher and author of *Channeling: Investigations on Receiving Information from Paranormal Sources*, theorized:

> Perhaps God, the Universe, or All-That-Exists, is really something like a dissociated Being, a multiple personality, as experienced from our perspective as Its own dissociated subpersonalities. All aspects of Creation are in an evolutionary process of overcoming this "cosmological dissociation." As part of this overcoming process, we are learning to transmute our condition of relative disconnectedness and to access ever more of the omniscience, omnipotence, omnipresence, and omnibenevolence of our common Universal Being. Unfortunately, at this stage of our evolution, much of the energy and information involved in such accessing is being condescendingly perceived as somehow sub-real or unreal, as only imaginational, delusional, mystical, magical, or paranormal in nature, whereas it is in actuality manifestations of a deeper truth and a greater reality.

I cannot help but urge every writer I meet to consider the possibility of a reality much greater than ourselves, one that is not limited by time, space, the five senses, or any of the physical laws we understand. Moreover, we are inexplicably at-one with this greater reality, not cut off from it by the outer layer of skin and bone that defines our physical bodies. We awaken to this greater reality and draw from it for our creative inspiration, not by sequestering ourselves away in the proverbial garret to do our writing, burdened by the belief that we are all alone in the creative act, but by opening ourselves up to the possibility that we can ask for and get assistance from this invisible reality. This can be done through a channeled inner guide or live psychic readings where we can experience the power of the synergy between author and listener that the ancient oral storytellers knew so well, or through prayer, or by entering altered states of consciousness from a variety of means. The act of writing itself places us in a non-ordinary state of consciousness, wherein this other reality is just a short journey away.

Let's go there!

WRITING EXPLORATION #11
MUSES, INNER GUIDES,
AND SPIRIT TEACHERS

Many writers have a personal muse. They might not think of it this way or call it a muse because the person who is acting in this role for them is a real person, perhaps a parent, grandparent, or close friend, who encouraged them to write, who told them stories, or read to them when they were a small child. Because this is the memory of a real person, the writer doesn't think of this as an unusual experience — which it isn't. However, the fact remains that this memory is the source of real inspiration and strength, even when that muse person is not physically present.

Other people are inspired by authors, dead or alive, whose work they admire or by mythological figures, heroes, or heroines from novels, movies, or plays. And still others have muses who come into their consciousness spontaneously and do not have a complement in real life.

If you have a muse or inner guide in any form — an actual person who inspired you, an author, a legendary hero/heroine, a fictional character, etc. — do this:

1. Get a clear picture of them in your mind.
2. Imagine what it would be like to experience the world

through that person's mind. Think about what they have experienced in their life, how they perceive you, their critical capacities, and their relationship with you.

3. Now read something you have written but read it as though you are no longer yourself but this other person who is to be your muse or guide.

4. After this reading, write down your responses as if you were this other person, writing a letter to the author (you). As you are doing this, do your very best to stay in character, that is, seeing the writing through the mind of your muse. In your writing as this person, compliment the writing where you honestly feel it deserves it, make suggestions for improving it, and offer any further information you feel the author needs to knows.

5. Come out of character and return to your everyday state of mind.

Do this exercise once or twice a week for several weeks. Then experiment with this inner voice, seeking its opinion on your writing. Ask it for assistance on any issue that you might ask a writing coach.

Just as in creating a character for a fictional work, this muse or inner guide will increasingly take on a life of its own the more you use it. But always remember, no matter what it might tell you, you are the final judge and jury. Don't change a line, no matter what your muse tells you, unless it feels exactly right to you.

CHAPTER TWELVE

Creating a System
of Supportive Critiquing

An artist who theorizes about his work is no longer artist but critic.

— H. G. Wells

In teaching writing seminars, I've heard many stories about people being psychologically ground up by informal writers' groups. There seem to be built-in hazards with these groups, based on some rather widespread misunderstandings about the role of criticism in the creative process. While I am certainly not against criticism, I also know that the creative spirit in each of us can be fragile and impressionable. Our creativity has a life of its own and must be treated with care, particularly in its infancy. Whether you're twenty-six or forty or seventy-five, if you have just started taking your creative life seriously, your creativity is an infant and must be treated accordingly. As it grows, parent it carefully and avoid insensitive critics, just as you would avoid cigarettes and abusive people when you are pregnant. The parallels between giving birth to your creativity and giving birth to a child are much closer than you might think. And if you are a man, you'll just have to imagine this — as I do. During your creativity's infancy, nourish it well and shield it from abuse.

Every writers' group seems to include at least one published writer who feels it necessary to appoint himself or herself the resident expert. This person harangues other members of the group with his or her opinions about what constitutes good writing and what each person should do to improve. This criticism really serves to bolster his or her own ego, not to nurture the other writers' gestating creative spirits. Like an abusive parent, this self-appointed critic's bombast stifles growth and undermines the self-trust so essential for creative growth.

It is important to give feedback, of course, but what concerns me more than anything else is how to do that supportively in a writers' group. Or if you are sharing writings with a friend, how does the friend give you nurturing and honest feedback, something that will help you grow your creative child rather than just force it into adulthood all too soon. These questions have been particularly important for me to answer because my way of teaching writing is very different from most. Primarily, my teaching is based not on comparisons to others' work but on the new author's own inner gifts and intents.

In the following pages, I describe a system for giving feedback that is nourishing and supportive, fostering the principles I have talked about in this book. This method is easily applied both when working alone and when developing a constructive and supportive writers' group. The goal throughout is to develop ways to evaluate creative work while fully acknowledging the author's original intent and gifts even as you are expanding everyone's awareness of how to communicate well. Put another way, this form of critiquing asks how we can help each other expand our creative gifts while fully respecting the fact that as powerful as creativity is, it is also as fragile as life itself.

TWO KINDS OF FEEDBACK

There are two kinds of feedback, one ego-driven and destructive, the other supportive and constructive:

- **"Judgmatic" Criticism.** (Destructive) This kind of feedback often marches under the banner of the "democratic process," based on the belief that everyone is entitled to their own opinion. Feedback is composed of (a) how much the person giving feedback likes the piece, (b) how it compares to "great literature," (c) how it compares with a book the critic has recently read, and (d) how the work being criticized aligns with the critic-of-the-moment's way of seeing things. Little or no concern goes into looking at the piece on its own terms or understanding the importance of treating the gestating creative spirit with respect for its present level of development.

- **Benchmark Feedback.** (Constructive) By its very nature, each creative work is unique, and the goal of feedback should be to fully draw out that uniqueness. Benchmark feedback starts with a statement about how the piece affects the reader on a human level. My own experience as a seminar teacher, coach, and author has convinced me that if you take the time to pay attention to what produces the greatest human impact, you will be led to the skills and techniques that best apply to your particular creative gift. Unfortunately, and most commonly, creative writing teachers use writing techniques as a formula for writing well, which pretty much guarantees that you won't discover your own voice.

The idea of a benchmark is twofold: First, the term was used by early artisans, such as silversmiths, clock makers, and potters, to indicate a certain set of standards established by the artisan him- or herself. To find the "signature" of this or that artisan on a piece of work was seen as a kind of assurance that the piece met the standards, or benchmark, of that particular artisan.

The term also means to designate a starting point, as in establishing a cornerstone for the construction of a building. That point provides the reference point for all the work that comes after. This ensures the integrity of the whole structure. Here the idea of a benchmark in critiquing our own or another person's creative work means that we need to pay homage to the fact that everyone's starting point is a little different. Any effort to help that person build and grow must be done with clear reference to their particular cornerstone.

Artistic feedback is most productive when we patiently and tenaciously discipline ourselves around the issue of human impact. Beyond that, it is important to clearly articulate benchmarks that each and every person in the writers' group understands and agrees upon. This includes having sessions to discuss the kinds of criteria you will adopt. The most important part of this process is clearly articulating a set of criteria that everyone understands, so that people receiving feedback can more easily decide whether or not the feedback they are getting is relevant.

As you consider my suggestions in the following pages, I have one warning: Don't use my list of benchmarks as rules for writing well. It doesn't work that way. Rather, the ideas I am outlining here compose a way of paying attention, of listening well. Forget everything on this list while you are writing.

CRITIQUE WITH SUPPORTIVE WISDOM

When giving feedback on another person's manuscript, or while evaluating your own work, look at it in terms of the criteria listed on pages 202–203. Give feedback only for the areas where these criteria are working. If you don't feel any of them are working, don't comment. The purpose of this kind of feedback is to seek in each other's work models for effective writing. Be very careful about telling other people how to "fix things" that, within the bigger picture of their overall development as a writer, "ain't broke."

Comment on areas that are weak *only* if the person specifically asks for that feedback. Then do so only after they have stated what they understand about the criteria in question.

Note that this list is not numbered. No hierarchy is intended or implied.

This feedback sheet is intended as a temporary guideline for looking at your own work, or for reading or listening to others' writing and providing feedback. I designed it to broaden your understanding of what works and what you might build upon. Think of this sheet as a supplement to appreciative listening and feedback, which are the key principles of the *Write from the Heart* approach to creativity.

Avoid thinking of this as a "rating sheet." As you become familiar with the various benchmarks outlined here — and then listen to, read, and are moved by your own or someone else's writing — you can begin to articulate which of these benchmarks capture your attention and help you. Build on those, rather than focusing on benchmarks that are not working as well.

Here are a couple of examples:

- The depth of an author's self-disclosure might have moved you, and you note this on the feedback sheet.

- If you felt the author established a particularly close connection with the reader, you would identify this as an
  "intimacy" benchmark and build on that strength by
  telling them what in their writing touched you.

While you will discover many different purposes for the
Benchmark Feedback Sheet as you become familiar with it, its
main purposes are

- To sensitize authors to what produces the most powerful
  impact on readers.
- To provide a vocabulary for enhancing our thinking
  about and discussion of written material.
- To provide a unifying map and a common language (particularly in writers' groups) for receiving and giving feedback.
- To help you appraise your own writing, identify your
  strengths, and recognize what you should further
  emphasize in your own writing.
- To specify areas of criticism. In presenting your own
  writing, you can use these criteria for requesting specific
  help. For example, you might say, "I want to have a
  strong sense of connecting with the reader in this piece,
  but I'm not certain if I've accomplished that. Could I
  read it and get your feedback on that point?"
- To help writers identify their real strengths and what their
  present strengths or gifts really are. For example, a writer
  might think she wants to express universal themes, but

listeners and readers might identify that where she has the greatest impact is through the simple beauty of her writing.

BENCHMARK FEEDBACK SHEET: THE BASIC CRITERIA

The following questions are written from the perspective of the reader or listener. If you are using this list to critique your own work, do so from the point of view that you are the reader, not the writer of the piece you are evaluating.

- **Human Impact.** How does the piece affect you on a strictly human and personal level? Point out a specific part of the piece that impacted you and tell why it did.
- **Intimacy.** Did you feel that the author was aware of your presence as the reader? Specify what in the writing made you feel the author was aware of you.
- **Author Disclosure.** Do you feel close to the author, that you know who they are? Point out places in the piece where the author revealed him- or herself to you.
- **Authenticity & Passion.** What made you feel that the author really knew and cared about what she or he was writing about?
- **Voice.** Does the writing seem to come out of the author's own life experience? What specifically convinces you of this?

- **Beauty.** Does the piece have that elusive value we call "beauty," and if it does, specify where and how this was communicated.
- **Authority.** Can you hear the author's strength? Do they stand in their own power? Identify a specific line or lines where this occurs.
- **Form.** Does the piece have a clear sense of "form" — a beginning, middle, and end?
- **Universality.** Does it strike a chord for you? Does it cause an "ah-ha!" reaction in you? Describe how it did this.
- **Relevance.** In what way is the piece useful to you? Remember that this can include anything from giving practical instructions to entertaining and delighting you.
- **Transformation.** Does the piece take you from one frame of mind or way of experiencing the world to another? Describe the way it does this.
- **Holographic Effect.** Do all the pieces seem to reflect the whole? What is it that gives you the impression that this is true?
- **Immersion.** How deeply do you feel involved or immersed in the piece? How does the author achieve this?

CHAPTER THIRTEEN

Getting
Happily Published

Even though so much of my writing time is stressful and disheartening,
I carry a secret sense of accomplishment around with me,
like a radium pack implanted near my heart that now leaches
a quiet sense of relief through my system.

— Anne Lamott

While putting the finishing touches on this book, I was reminded that one of the most frequently asked questions in any group of young writers is, "How do I get published?" The short answer is, "Write something that publishers want." While that may sound flippant, I have to say that there is more than a bit of truth in it. I'm always having to remind myself that while most authors write to satisfy a deep inner need, most publishers publish to make money. I'm not saying they're unprincipled money-grubbers whose only motive is profit. In fact, most of the people I know in publishing — editors, marketing and publicity people, and even sales reps

— have a genuine love for books. Overall, there are probably more really good people, people of integrity and high ideals, in publishing than in any other major industry.

Keeping a publishing company afloat means you've got to sell books, and that means that you better develop a good eye for manuscripts that are going to stir up some excitement in the marketplace. As authors we should be grateful that somebody looks out for the money end of publishing. God knows, writers aren't very good at that.

Don't get me wrong. I don't think that writers should write what they think publishers or even their readers want. On the contrary! If there's a single ingredient publishers look for in that stack of manuscripts that comes in over the transom every month, it's got something to do with how deeply the author is enmeshed in his or her work. When the author is passionately involved, that passion comes across with every word, and it turns readers on. In that respect, we could probably draw some real parallels between writing and making love. I mean there's nothing quite so gloomy as trying to do either one with a partner whose heart isn't in it.

When I was first starting to get published, I asked an editor from a large New York publishing house what she looked for in a manuscript. She told me, "I'm looking for writing that comes from the heart, books that are written because the author *has* to write them. If that deep involvement is there, I'll work with the author until we produce something that's publishable. I don't care what the subject is as long as this rare ingredient is present."

I'm not sure that every publisher thinks this way but I like what this editor says. While a good acquisitions editor keeps an eye focused on current trends, they also know that it's impossible to predict what's going to be a best-seller a year from now, which is about the shortest time it will take the writer and the publisher to get a book out. Knowing that nobody has twenty-twenty vision when it comes to predicting what's going to sell next year, the smart editors look for new ideas and the author's passion.

Why is the author's passion for the material so important to editors and readers? I contend it's the same reason that magazines like *People* and *Us* are so popular — we all take a kind of voyeuristic delight in looking at the world through another person's eyes. We're not just curious about how others live; it's more than that. We really want to get outside ourselves and look at life in a different way. We want to get over ourselves, to perhaps discover and enjoy a part of life we had overlooked. Readers are generally pretty voracious about wanting to get more out of life, and when they're seeking that, the author's passion draws them in like a powerful magnet.

All this is well and good, but how do you get a publisher to even look at your manuscript? The truth is that most of the large publishers — houses like Random House, Doubleday, HarperCollins, Simon & Schuster — won't look at unsolicited manuscripts. That's shorthand for "I'll only look at manuscripts that a literary agent has brought to me." And what do they do with the unsolicited ones? I got a wonderful object lesson about this nearly twenty years ago when I flew back to New York to meet with an editor there.

This was at one of the largest publishing houses in the city. I took the elevator up to the tenth floor and when the doors opened, I found myself facing a bored receptionist, barely visible behind a large pile of manuscripts. She took my name, repeated it into her intercom, and told me to take a seat. Meanwhile, she proceeded to open the big envelopes on her desk, flip through them, then stuff them into other envelopes and toss them into a plastic mail container on the floor. I would guess that she actually riffled through the pages of every fifth or sixth manuscript. I asked her, "What's in all those envelopes?"

"Manuscripts people send," she replied, listlessly. "We get a whole stack of them every day."

"Are you the main person who reads them?" I asked.

"I don't really read them," she said. "Sometimes I glance through one or two if they look interesting."

"And what makes a manuscript look interesting?"

"Oh, I don't know. Sometimes a title. Sometimes just the fact that it's nicely printed out. I can't really say."

Writers are always a great nuisance to publishers. If they could do without them, they would.

— Fay Weldon

I was speechless. I thought about all the manuscripts I'd sent out in my day, before I had an agent. And I quickly calculated how much money I had contributed to the U.S. Postal Service, to say nothing of the copy services near my home, to have this person or her counterpart in other companies go through this little ritual. Roughly estimating the number of unagented freelance writers in the United States, I concluded that their contribution alone could support pensions for the entire postal service!

FINDING AN AGENT

The next most logical question is, "How do I get an agent so that my work can move beyond the status of the unsolicited manuscript?" And the answer to that is the same one I gave in answer to the question, "How do I get published?" Only more so. I say more so because agents are salespeople. That's their job. A person becomes a successful agent for one reason only: They consistently deliver to publishers manuscripts that require minimal editing and sell well after they're made into books.

Now comes another frustration to make you a little more crazy than you already are: Chances are that any agent who's been around for a while is going to tell you they don't look at authors who haven't previously published. So you're down in the sand trap again because you haven't been published before...and if you had been you probably wouldn't be worrying about how to get an agent.

Remember I said that *successful agents who've been around*

Before agents and publishers will accept a work of fiction (especially from a newer writer), they require a complete manuscript. However, nonfiction projects are different: A proposal alone can do the trick. This is what makes nonfiction writing a much less speculative and often more lucrative endeavor (relatively speaking) than fiction writing.

— Jeff Herman

for a while don't take on unpublished authors. However, that's just one category of agents. The other category is the agent who is just starting out and is looking desperately for some good properties to handle. These folks are in a position very similar to your own: They want to be agents but all the successful published authors already have agents. So they need you as much as you need them. And just because they're new in the business doesn't mean they can't do a good job for you, any more than your not being published yet means you're not a good writer.

Most literary agents are people who have worked in publishing, usually as editors. They might have (a) lost their jobs through downsizing of the company or because somebody didn't like them, or (b) gotten sick and tired of working long hours in-house for too little pay and wanted to be their own boss. They are often people who have been around publishing enough that they've built up some good contacts and know how to get a foot in the door of at least a couple of major publishers.

But how do you meet these people? If you live in or near a large city, you will probably know of a writers' club or a place where writers' workshops are given. Agents who are just starting out frequently go to such places looking for new clients. So keep an eye out for them; they may be presenting a class on publishing or simply announcing their presence at regular meetings. They may even be members of writers' clubs, which they join to scout for new clients.

You will also find listings for literary agents in two key writers' reference guides: *Literary Market Place (LMP)* and the annual *Guide to Literary Agents* published by Writer's Digest Books. Both of these sources provide descriptions of agents, the genres they specialize in, whether or not they take on new writers, and of course, where they can be reached.

I'd also highly recommend subscribing to *Publishers Weekly,* which is essentially the publishing industry's trade journal. In addition, join NAPRA (Networking Alternatives for Publishers, Retailers, and Artists, Inc.) and get their magazine, with reviews on most recent offerings from independent publishers. Between these two sources you'll get all the inside information on what publishers, editors, and agents are doing — plus book reviews, author interviews, forecasts, and the ever popular best-seller lists. In the back of each weekly magazine you'll also find classified ads, with an occasional notice of new literary agencies starting up. Although reading it each week can be maddening — particularly when you hear about the latest multimillion-dollar advance to a romance novelist who you're certain isn't half as deserving as you. (See the bibliography for information concerning NAPRA and *Publisher's Weekly.*)

The best way to approach an agent is through a short query letter describing your project. By short I mean a single page, with one paragraph describing your book and a second one telling a little about yourself. For example, if you are writing a book on a medical subject, you'd either want to give your own medical credentials or tell about a coauthor who has these credentials. If your book is a novel or collection of poems, then formal credentials are probably not going to be as relevant. Don't make the mistake of getting too chatty and cute, either; agents and editors really don't care if you have a bullterrier named Sherwood (after the author Sherwood Anderson) and a Persian cat named Zelda (after F. Scott Fitzgerald's wife) who snuggles up on top of your computer monitor when you write.

In your cover letter, try to avoid "hyping" either your book or yourself. One of the banes of every agent and editor is having to deal with temperamental authors and their overblown egos — not that you or I would ever be guilty of such an impropriety! Too much hype in a cover letter is like waving a red flag. So stick to business and get to the point as quickly and cleanly as you can. Query letters are important, and there's an art to writing really good ones. For further help with this, a number of books are available for writing query letters, one of which you'll find cited in the bibliography.

One of the best ways for a beginning writer to get an agent or a publisher is to get a referral by a friend who is a published writer. But not all of us can boast of having such a person in our collection of friends. Regardless, keep your eyes open for any opportunity to connect with other writers who might be interested in your project. For example, let's say you take a workshop from an author who is writing something similar to your writing. Once you've taken his or her class and gotten to know them a bit, simply ask if they can recommend an agent or publisher to you. Ask if they'd consider taking a look at your manuscript, with the possibility of giving you a referral to their own agent or publisher. Most authors are open to this; others make it their policy never to stick their necks out in this way. But don't be afraid to ask.

When you're shopping around for a publisher or agent, remember that most of them tend to specialize in particular kinds of books. For example, some publishers only want to see mystery novels. Others want to see only nonfiction, say, biographies and popular sociology. Do some research before you query anybody. Make certain you are sending your letters to people who work with the genre in which you're writing. The best way to find this out is to browse *Literary Market Place, Writer's Market,* and listings of agents.

ABOUT BOOK PROPOSALS

In the past twenty years, most nonfiction books have been sold to publishers on the basis of a selling proposal. This is a description of your book, presented in what has by now become a fairly standardized format. (See *Write the Perfect Book Proposal* in the bibliography.) Publishers give an advance against royalties based on this proposal, giving the author the financial resources they'll need to complete the manuscript. Advances of this kind run from a few hundred dollars up to the millions, depending on the potential salability of the finished project.

Elements of a Book Proposal

1. Title page
2. Overview
3. Author background
4. Competitive or complementary books
5. Who will buy the book
6. Promotional plan
7. Chapter outline
8. Sample chapters (usually two)
9. Additional material that will help convince a publisher that your project and you will make them money

I have never known of a first-time fiction writer who could sell a book on the basis of a proposal. But this is not to say that it never happens. If you're a fiction writer, count on having to present a finished manuscript to your agent. Once you've had a couple of bestsellers, you can probably talk to your publisher about an advance based on a new book idea.

A WORD ABOUT
THE STATUS OF WRITERS

Most of us who still revere books also think of authors as special people. Even a minor poet in a small town can be a celebrity. But within big-time publishing, the author is just one cog in the complex gearing of a very complicated machine. The day you turn over your final draft to your editor, a whole chain of activities is set into motion. There are acquisition editors (your main contact with the publisher), line editors, copyeditors, publicity and marketing people, the accounting department, book designers, a cover artist, typesetters, binderies, warehouse workers, the catalog department, sales reps, booksellers, and finally, way down the line, the reader. As difficult as it might be to accept, you are just the supplier of the raw material for a product all these people will shape into the product called a book.

It's important for authors to keep some perspective on all this. Give the other people who are going to be involved with your book proper credit. Recognize that without their help you would never get your stuff into print.

Self-publishing is a perfect example of the American dream. It is stimulating, demanding, and rewarding. For many it has proved to be the do-it-yourself way to fame and fortune.

— Tom and Marilyn Ross

A little humility, patience, and a show of appreciation will go a long way. Eight years ago, I had a publishing experience that truly humbled me. My editor at one of New York's largest publishing houses called me one afternoon to share the following story.

Christine (not her real name) was coming to her office after lunch when she happened to drop by the publicity department where she worked. As she was walking through, she saw a huge stack of my new books, which were being mailed out to reviewers. Since Christine had not yet received a copy for herself she asked the publicist if she could have one.

"Not on your life," the publicist said. "These are all earmarked for our reviewers' list."

Somewhat miffed, my editor sputtered, "Are editors the last ones to get copies?!"

The publicist glanced at the ceiling, looked thoughtful, and then replied: "No. I believe the authors are."

I don't think there was any hostility in this answer. The publicist was just stating a fact. Remember, few of the people who work on the editing and publishing of a book ever see or even talk to an author. They talk with each other, with their co-workers, but the author simply doesn't exist as a real person for them. Authors seldom visit their publishers, and in all the years I've been writing I have never had an editor introduce me to anyone else in the house — even when I went there in person to visit. In fact, I would not even recognize most of the editors of the more than two hundred books I've been involved with. Particularly when a publisher is across the country, way over on the other coast, your only contact with them will be by phone or letter. And by the way, editors don't win any awards for returning phone calls.

In the broad scheme of things, it's important to see where we writers fit in. Even though the industry is dependent on the raw material we provide, we're also only semi-visible to most of the people who do what's necessary to transform our manuscripts into books and get them into the marketplace. If we're to be happily published, we need to know how to stick up for ourselves but we also need to give credit where it's due. This means sending signed copies of your book, with a short note of appreciation, to your editor and any other people you've had any kind of contact with in the process of getting your work out. And it also means joining a writers' union, such as the Authors Guild (see the bibliography), which can act as your advocate in those rare times when you will need one.

MAJOR PUBLISHERS VERSUS THE NEW INDEPENDENTS

In the past twenty years, there have been some major changes in book publishing that every new writer should understand before submitting a manuscript. The best way to describe these changes is to look at the publisher of the book you are holding in your hands. New World Library is a good example of what has come to be known in the industry as an independent publisher.

The company was the brainstorm of Marc Allen, who wanted

to take on book projects that he felt could be helpful to people committed to a path of personal and spiritual development. In this respect, New World Library's focus is a broad one, with millions of readers.

In today's publishing world, independent publishing is a significant force. The companies can be small (one or two new books per year) or large (a dozen or more books per year), serving authors and a readership that for the most part the large New York publishing houses have abandoned. To understand why this is so, one should know a little about publishing history. So let's go back a bit.

Until the late 1960s, most of the New York publishers were family run, and across the board this industry got along on very narrow profit margins. Editorial policies were very loose. Most of these houses published what personally appealed to them or their editors. If a book sold three thousand copies but made an important statement, it was considered a success. Then, larger conglomerates, mainly Hollywood and New York media interests, started buying out book publishers, and at this point the "bottom line" and good profits became more important than publishing quality work. Today, New York publishing is best-seller driven and every editor is looking for best-sellers first and message books or good literature second.

When New York started chasing after best-sellers, some excellent books went begging. As a result, the industry suddenly broke off onto a new path — giving rise to the small, independent publisher, usually controlled by a single person much as New York publishing was in its infancy.

In the beginning, the new independents had a hard time of it. They acquired and published excellent material but they lacked the distribution channels to get their products into the marketplace. And obviously, having a garage or a warehouse full of books without any effective way to get them into the bookstores wasn't working to anyone's benefit. To answer this need, independent distributors began cropping up all over the country, companies like Bookpeople, New Leaf, and Publishers Group West, to name just a few.

The new distributors handled mostly small, independent publishers. They provided cataloging and shipping services, which got the books into the stores. But some of these distributors were local businesses, serving bookstores in one or two states. They also lacked book reps, that is, salespeople who went into the stores, talked to booksellers, checked out how their books were being displayed, and got their products recognized. Most independent distributors and publishers depended on booksellers ordering from catalogs, which were simply alphabetized lists of many different publishers' offerings.

In the 1980s, independent distributors went a step further, building into their lists of services sales reps who made personal contact with booksellers, consulting for independent publishers on how to better promote their books, advertisements in trade journals, and catalogs that served publishers and booksellers in ways comparable to the big New York publishers. Today, this new brand of book distributor has made it possible for niche publishers to compete with even the biggest New York publishers. What's more, the best of the independents are now getting out books that are themselves best-sellers, that is, single titles that sell in the hundreds of thousands, or even millions of copies, just like their giant New York counterparts' books.

For the beginning writer, the new independents are generally more approachable than the larger New York houses. Most will read unsolicited manuscripts, and many of them prefer dealing directly with authors rather than going through agents. Also, they give more personal help. On the downside, most independents don't have the big budgets that the larger houses do, so don't expect a huge advance. But there are trade-offs that can more than make up for the difference, particularly for writers who haven't yet established a track record. Because they must have something to attract writers, the independents offer more personal contact with their authors, giving editorial help similar to what New York houses used to give in the 1920s and 1930s. People in publishing tend to forget that in the era of the Great American Novel, when literary giants such as Ernest Hemingway, F. Scott Fitzgerald, Katherine Ann Porter, William Faulkner, Lillian Hellman, and Sherwood Anderson came along, some gifted editors, notably Maxwell Perkins, brought these authors along. While it is now rare for a large New York house to put a lot of effort into developing their authors, this tradition of the developmental editor is still very much alive with many independents.

Besides offering editorial support, the independent publisher tends to get books out a little sooner than the larger houses. An independent who's on top of things can get a book out within six months of receiving a finished manuscript; with a larger house, you're looking at getting books in a year and a half or more. What this means to you is that your book starts earning money for you up to a year sooner with an independent publisher.

Another selling point to consider with independent publishers is that they must make every book count. They buy books that will "backlist," that is, books that will have a long life — ten years or more, in many cases. This can mean a lot to you over time. For example, a small independent called Bookworks, whose books were distributed by Random House in New York, published my book *The Well Body Book.* In its first year that book sold twenty thousand copies. But it stayed in print for ten years, getting into print in several other countries, for total sales of over a quarter of a million copies. With a larger New York house, it might not have stayed in print so long.

SHORTER PATHS TO PUBLICATION

Since the first edition of this book, way back in 1995, printing technologies have changed dramatically; also, the Internet has created opportunities for authors to publish. These technologies continue to change at such a rapid rate that keeping up with them is nearly impossible. The best way I can serve readers is to discuss present trends and new opportunities with the caveat that by the time you read this book there will have been further changes beyond what anyone can imagine. I'm sure that with the following notes, your access to the Internet, and a little detective work, you can pursue later developments on your own. I am confident that the following will at least provide you with questions to lead you to the answers you seek.

Never before in history has publishing a book been easier or more affordable. As late as 1996, it was not economically feasible to print less than three thousand copies of a book. With setup costs being the same for a few hundred as for many thousands of copies, the cost per book obviously goes down significantly the more you print. The cost of printing only five hundred or a thousand books used to mean that if you sold your book through wholesalers, you'd lose money. However, by printing three thousand copies, many self-publishers, without the knowledge, inner spark, or expertise necessary to publicize their work, or even get books into bookstores, ended up with a pallet of unsold books in their garages.

Today's printing technologies, backed up by the personal computer, completely change this picture. Now an author or first-time publisher can print as few as three hundred copies of a book and still have enough of a margin to make a little money. Print runs of even five hundred copies can be quite profitable for a writer who lectures and teaches workshops and sells their books in the back of the room. I know of one author, who lectures on self-care medical subjects, who sells her 350-page, very technical nutrition book in the back of the room for forty dollars. That's nearly ten times what it costs her to print it. It is not unusual, by the way, for technical and professional books to carry such a high price because the purchaser is paying for specialized expertise not otherwise available.

In consulting with first-time self-publishers, I recommend that unless they have a "sure thing," of which there are very few in this business, they should publish no more than 1,500 copies the first time around. Look at the first printing as a market test, and if it turns out that you get a scathing review that discourages sales, you won't be out a lot of money. Also, readers often find errors you didn't catch and the smaller numbers for your first print run mean you can correct your errors next time around. If you are seriously considering self-publishing, keep in mind that most people can sell five hundred books to their own circle of friends, acquaintances, and local bookstores. If the book takes off, most printers can simply set up the presses again and have another three thousand or more books off to you in a few weeks.

Is it difficult to publish your own book? Not half as difficult as you might think. Thanks to computers and an increased number of author-friendly printers, good freelance editors, book designers, and production editors, self-publishing is a lot less difficult than writing the manuscript in the first place. And if you know enough about computers to write your book on one, you can also format the entire manuscript to make a great-looking book and thus save the two thousand to three thousand dollars you might otherwise spend to have a typesetter do it. Printers who specialize in working with first-time publishers often will supply templates or other instructions for formatting, and some even design simple book covers.

Costs for printing a thousand 200-page, quality paperback

books, with full-color covers, should be around $3.25 per book, or $3,250 total. On top of that you will have to figure in the design of a cover (if you don't do it yourself), shipping, and any editorial help you might choose to hire. Such a book would retail for about $12. (Bookstores get a 30- to 40-percent discount, so factor that in.)

But there are still other options to think about. At the time of this writing, handheld electronic readers, called e-books, offer a whole new way to produce and read books. Electronic files of books can be purchased over the Internet and downloaded to your e-book reader. You can then snuggle up with your electronic reader and enjoy a good read. An ever-increasing number of publishers offer books on the Internet in this format. Or with software to make computer reading more enjoyable, you can read books on your laptop computer.

Online services selling e-books display graphics of the cover, a description of the book, and sometimes a sample chapter or two to browse. As an author, you submit your manuscript as you would to any publisher, except that you do so electronically. In some cases, e-book publishers are so anxious to get manuscripts that they will produce your book and advertise it online for free. In other cases, you pay a nominal fee (usually under five hundred dollars). As more publishers adopt this technology, we will probably find them following editorial practices akin to the paper book tradition, with a panel of editors deciding what they will or will not publish.

Finally, there is the new technology known as print-on-demand or POD, which means that you print out books only as you get orders for them — even if it is just a single copy. The book comes to you as a quality paperback, usually with a full-color cover. At least two Internet companies offer an excellent package for doing this. You sign up to work with them for a fee under five hundred dollars, and they advertise your book on their website, collect payment, and print out and ship books as they receive orders. They pay you 20 percent of whatever they get for the book. That's $2.40 in royalties on a $12 book. If you want to order a batch of books to have on hand, you can buy them from the company for 20 to 30 percent off, depending on how many you order at a time.

Some of the same companies also handle electronic formats, with people ordering your book for their handheld electronic readers. In that case, the book retails for about two dollars less than the paper version but you get 50 percent royalties! (These figures may vary.) Not bad when you consider that most traditional publishers pay only 7.5 percent — half that if they are selling your books at deep discounts such as to book clubs, discount clubs, and special markets.

The online companies that produce POD books also list your book with the big online bookstores and with certain chain stores, just as a more traditional publisher would do. So your self-published work could possibly reach millions of people. Granted, you don't have the editorial or promotional support you might get with a regular publisher, but keep in mind that unless your book is a bestseller, most regular publishers won't assign a very large promotional budget to your project anyway.

Publishing is becoming increasingly democratic, thanks to

author-friendly printers, the Internet, POD, and the advent of the e-book. While there are those who say that e-books will never replace paper books, my vision is that the market for such books is soon to undergo some major changes. At the time of this writing, according to a news report, Time Warner is entering the e-book business, pushed in part by Microsoft's announcement of software and an electronic reading device that make reading books this way far more appealing than ever before.

I believe that certain books, perhaps those we associate with taking to the beach or curling up with in front of the fireplace, will stay in the more traditional paper form. The cover design, the feeling of the paper, and even the weight of the paper in your hand are all important parts of these reading experiences. But I have no doubt that we will in the very near future see e-books emerging as a viable force in publishing, and many genres, most notably technical manuals and reference books, will naturally gravitate toward this publishing medium.

There are many things to be said in favor of e-books. Certainly this is a cheaper, faster, and more environmentally friendly way to publish. The advantage for first-time authors is tremendous because publishers won't have to risk as large an investment of their time and money to bring a new author to market. Moreover, the e-book combined with Internet opportunities means that authors can self-publish and reach a large potential readership on their own. I'm all for electronic publishing, if only because it empowers authors and makes a broader range of written material available to us all.

Even at the time of this writing, which is fairly early in the e-book revolution, many mainstream publishers are making books available to e-book readers. And best-selling authors are embracing the medium enthusiastically. The big news in 2000 was Stephen King making his book *Riding the Bullet* available in the e-book format exclusively — at least the first half of the book could be read for *free!* And many magazines, notably *Esquire* and *Fast Company,* are also available in e-book formats.

Distribution for e-books is already broad. The major online chain stores such as Barnes & Noble and Amazon.com have announced that they will carry a significant line of e-books. And large independent bookstores, such as the legendary Powell's Books in Portland, Oregon, carry them on their online sites.

The writing is on the wall — or at least on your computer monitor. E-books are fast becoming a viable contender in the world of publishing. There's still some resistance to them, with many traditional book lovers screaming that the new technology will never replace the cozy thought of curling up with a good book — a paper book. But let's keep in mind that there was a similar outcry not so long ago from writers who swore that they would never abandon their beloved typewriters for computers. My wife likes to remind me that I was one of them! And when I go back to the typewriter, which we keep around for addressing oversized envelopes, I can barely use the thing.

Whatever your future as an author, explore all the avenues available for publishing your work. If you publish your first book as an e-book, that doesn't preclude the possibility of publishing it in other formats or even having a major publisher pick it up. It doesn't take a great prophet to see that the e-book may still be in its infancy, but it is growing up fast and has already become a major worry to the more traditional publishers. It just might be your inroad to a highly successful publishing career.

ABOUT PUBLICITY

I think every published writer in the world complains that their publishers don't do enough to promote their books. We all blame our publishers for the fact that our treasured work didn't become a best-seller. But the truth is that the best advertising for any book is itself. Books are probably the most word-of-mouth product in the world. Although there are exceptions, a book sells because its readers are excited about it and want their friends to read it too. Readers themselves broadcast their enthusiasm and this, more than anything else, sells books.

Print advertising is expensive. To earn back the cost of a single ad in the *New York Times*, a publisher has to sell more than a thousand books. However, single ads barely get recognized. So if you're going to make it work at all you have to buy at least six ads, and then you're talking about big money. You'll have to sell five thousand books to earn back that kind of advertising expense. Considering that the average book only sells about that many copies, advertising simply isn't an economically viable way to promote books. There's a joke in the publishing world that really isn't a joke — that the only books that get any promotion to speak of are books that don't need it, those by celebrity authors or novelists whose books sell in the hundreds of thousands with or without advertising.

What does work then? How do books even find their way to their readers? A standard promotion for most publishers consists of sending out a batch of books to book reviewers for newspapers and magazines all over the country. A reviewers' list can have anywhere from 150 to 500 individuals, depending on the subject matter. In addition, your publisher should also send out press releases to radio and TV broadcasters, hoping that some of them will be interested enough in your work to either talk about you and your work or have you on their program as a guest. Aside from that, your publisher should make certain that the book rep, that is, the person who visits and takes orders from booksellers, knows about your book. Publishers hold sales conferences, insiders' events that authors are rarely invited to attend, to inform sales reps about their new books. And finally, they display your book at either BookExpo America, the big annual publishing event that thousands of publishers and booksellers attend, or regional bookseller association conferences throughout the country. A picture and a description of your book will also show up in the publisher's catalog and the catalogs of any distributors they might use.

The most powerful promotion of all, however, comes from you. For example, more and more booksellers are developing ongoing author appearance programs to have authors speak to their customers — and hopefully sign a stack of books that they can sell that night. You and your book would be advertised through the store and possibly the local newspapers. Readers love the opportunity to meet their favorite authors in person. You can always start the ball rolling by looking around your own neighborhood and contacting the owners of the bookstores you frequent. While most publishers will help you with all the details and will make certain there are books in stock for the night you appear, your personal contact with the bookseller is one of the greatest assets you have.

If your book lends itself to lectures or workshops, these are some of the best avenues of promotion. People will pay to attend functions such as these, and many authors make more money this way than they do selling books. The best thing about it is that you get paid for doing something that is good advertising for your book! For lectures, think of everything from service clubs to writers' workshops, wherever you fit in. Self-promotion of this kind can be a gold mine for writers who are willing to put themselves out there.

It's important for beginning writers to keep some perspective about writing. Publishing will probably not change your life. Few writers get rich or famous in today's world. But this way of life has rewards that you will find in very few other professions. So, writing is a golden grail definitely worth pursuing, with compensations that feed not just the pocketbook or your own ego, but something much more important than any of that — your very soul.

BIBLIOGRAPHY

CHAPTER ONE

Csikszentmihalyi, Mihaly. *Flow: The Psychology of Optimal Experience.* New York: Harper Perennial, 1991.

Kuhlewind, Georg. *Becoming Aware of the Logos.* New York: The Lindisfarne Press, 1985.

The New Oxford English Bible. Cambridge, Mass.: Oxford University Press, 1970.

CHAPTER TWO

Bennett, Hal Zina, and Michael Samuels. *The Well Body Book.* New York: Random House/Bookworks, 1972.

Stevens, Wallace. *The Necessary Angel.* New York: Random House, 1965.

Stevens, Wallace. *Collected Poems of Wallace Stevens.* New York: Vintage Books, 1990.

CHAPTER THREE

Whitehead, Alfred North. *Adventures of Ideas.* New York: Free Press, 1985.

Wordsworth, William. "I Wandered Lonely as a Cloud," *Selected Poetry* (Oxford World's Classics). Oxford: Oxford University Press, 1998.

CHAPTER FOUR

Emerson, Ralph Waldo. "Self Reliance," *The Essays of Ralph Waldo Emerson.* Cambridge, Mass.: Belknap Press/Harvard University Press, 1987.

CHAPTER FIVE

Osbon, Diane K., ed. *A Joseph Campbell Companion.* New York: HarperCollins, 1991.

CHAPTER SIX

Browning, Robert. "Saul," *The Collected Works of Robert Browning,* ed. Susan E. Dooley and Allan L. Dooley. Ohio University Press: 1999.

Keller, Helen. *The Story of My Life.* New York: Putnam, 1902.

CHAPTER SEVEN

Krishnamurti, J. *Meeting Life.* New York: HarperCollins, 1991.

Stevens, Wallace. "Peter Quince at the Clavier," *Collected Poems of Wallace Stevens.* New York: Vintage Books, 1990.

CHAPTER EIGHT

Jung, C. G. Recorded and edited by Aniela Jaffe. *Memories, Dreams, Reflections.* New York: Vintage Books, 1965.

CHAPTER NINE

Campbell, Joseph. *An Open Life.* Burdett, New York: Larsen Publications, 1988.

Faulkner, William. Nobel Prize Acceptance Speech, Stockholm, Sweden, December 10, 1950.

Nelson, Gertrud Mueller. *Here All Dwell Free.* New York: Doubleday, 1991.

CHAPTER TEN

Csikszentmihalyi, Mihaly. *Flow: The Psychology of Optimal Experience.* New York: Harper Perennial, 1991.

Stone, Hal and Sidra. *Embracing Our Selves: The Voice Dialogue Manual.* Novato, Calif.: Nataraj Publishing/New World Library, 1993.

CHAPTER ELEVEN

Bennett, Hal Zina. *The Lens of Perception.* Berkeley, Calif.: Celestial Arts/Ten Speed Press, 1993.

Kennedy, Eugene. "Earthwise: The Dawning of a New Spiritual Awareness." An interview with Joseph Campbell. *The New York Times Magazine,* April 15, 1979.

Hastings, Arthur. *With the Tongues of Men and Angels.* New York: Holt, Rinehart and Winston, 1991.

Jung, C.G. Recorded and edited by Aniela Jaffe. *Memories, Dreams, Reflections.* New York: Vintage Books, 1965.

Klimo, Jon. *Channeling: Investigations on Receiving Information from Paranormal Sources.* Los Angeles: Tarcher Books, 1987.

_____. "Cosmological Dissociation: Toward an Understanding of How We Create Reality." Proceedings of the Second International Conference on Paranormal Research. Fort Collins, Colorado, 1989.

O'Leary, Brian. *Exploring Inner and Outer Space.* Berkeley, Calif.: North Atlantic Books, 1989.

CHAPTER THIRTEEN

Cool, Lisa Collier. *How to Write Irresistible Query Letters.* Cincinnati, Ohio: Writer's Digest Books, 1991.

Guide to Literary Agents. Cincinnati, Ohio: Writer's Digest Books, annual.

Herman, Jeff. *Writer's Guide to Book Editors, Publishers, and*

Literary Agents, 2000–2001: Who They Are! What They Want! and How to Win Them Over. Rocklin, Calif.: Prima Publishing, 2000.

Herman, Jeff, and Deborah M. Adams. *Write the Perfect Book Proposal: Ten Proposals That Sold and Why.* New York: John Wiley & Sons, 1993.

Literary Market Place. New York: Bowker Publications, annual.

Publishers Weekly. Industry journal. For subscriptions, write 249 West 17th Street, New York, NY 10011.

Writer's Market. Cincinnati, Ohio: Writer's Digest Books, annual.

NAPRA ReView, for subscriptions, write NAPRA, 109 North Beach Road, P.O. Box 9, Eastbound, WA 98245-0009.

To join the Authors Guild, Inc., contact them at 330 West 42nd Street, New York, NY 10036; phone (212) 563-5904; fax (212) 564-5363; or www.authorsguild.org.

ABOUT THE AUTHOR

Hal Zina Bennett is the author of thirty fiction and nonfiction books. In addition to being a widely published author, he is one of the most sought-after creativity consultants and writing coaches in the country. His client list reads like a who's who of authors writing and lecturing in the fields of personal and spiritual development. He has helped more than two hundred authors develop their books for publication, a list that includes several best-sellers and at least three Oprah selections.

As a writing teacher, Hal has presented workshops, lectures, and classes at many leading institutions, including The Institute of

Transpersonal Psychology in Palo Alto, California, and The Omega Institute in Rhinebeck, New York. In the interest of bringing his special magic to as many young writers as possible, he and his wife, Susan J. Sparrow, founded *Write from the Heart Seminars* in 1994. They teach workshops throughout the United States. Hal and Susan also run a small publishing company, Tenacity Press. Hal's website is www.halzinabennett.com.

If you enjoyed *Write from the Heart,* we recommend the following books from New World Library:

Anybody Can Write: A Playful Approach by Roberta Jean Bryant. This book is a fun, user-friendly guide that is filled with great ideas to start you writing and keep you writing. It shows you how to relax and actually have fun writing, and how to discover the richness of your inner resources. It includes effective advice on how to get past the seven common types of writers' blocks. This book will help you finish the project you've been postponing.

Let the Crazy Child Write!: Finding Your Creative Writing Voice by Clive Matson. This book grew out of hundreds of creative writing workshops Clive Matson has led during his career as poet and writer. The book leads readers through a complete series of twelve seminars designed to help them find their creative writing voice. The book is a tool to be used, and readers are encouraged to work with at least one other person and create their own discussion group to work with the material.

Letters to a Young Poet by Rainer Maria Rilke. This luminous translation of Rainer Maria Rilke's classic offers brilliant inspiration to writers, artists, thinkers, and all people who seek to know and express their inner truth. *Letters to a Young Poet* is a classic that should be required reading for everyone who dreams of expressing themselves creatively.

Life — A User's Manual: Great Minds on the Big Questions edited by John Miller. Who am I? What am I doing here? Is there a God? What is life? This inspirational collection of short writings, quotes, and journal excerpts explores the joys, sorrows, and meanings of life — and helps provide some answers. Wise, profound, surprising, and entertaining, this elegantly produced book will offer instruction, insight, and inspiration to everyone looking for a sense of purpose in life.

The Soul of Creativity: Insights into the Creative Process edited by Tona Pearce Myers. In this wonderfully diverse collection of original writing, an extraordinary group of thinkers, teachers, and artists in many fields celebrate their personal experiences of creativity. It includes contributions from such notable writers as Diane Ackerman, Christina Baldwin, Hal Zina Bennett, Lucia Capacchione, Riane Eisler, Eric Maisel, John Fox, Jean Shinoda Bolen, SARK, and many more.

A Writer's Book of Days: A Spirited and Lively Muse for the Writing Life by Judy Reeves. This book offers writing practitioners 365 evocative writing topics guaranteed to keep the pen moving every day of the year. Writing topics are presented alongside bite-sized nuggets of information about writing practice: writing instructions, how-to's, monthly writing guidelines, bits of writing lore, and dozens of quotations and words of inspiration that entice and encourage the reader to keep writing.

New World Library is dedicated to
publishing books, audiocassettes, and videotapes
that inspire and challenge us to improve the quality
of our lives and our world.

Our books and tapes are available
in bookstores everywhere.
For a catalog of our complete library
of fine books and cassettes, contact:

New World Library
14 Pamaron Way
Novato, CA 94949

Phone: (415) 884-2100
Fax: (415) 884-2199
Or call toll-free (800) 972-6657
Catalog requests: Ext. 50
Ordering: Ext. 52

E-mail: escort@nwlib.com
Website: www.newworldlibrary.com